# Becoming a Contract Controller

→ Tips for a Thriving Career

 Ron Rael

## Notice to Readers

*Becoming a Contract Controller: Tips for a Thriving Career* does not represent an official position of the American Institute of Certified Public Accountants, and it is distributed with the understanding that the author and publisher are not rendering, legal, accounting, or other professional services in the publication. This book is intended to be an overview of the topics discussed within, and the author has made every attempt to verify the completeness and accuracy of the information herein. However, neither the author nor publisher can guarantee the applicability of the information found herein. If legal advice or other expert assistance is required, the services of a competent professional should be sought.

1 2 3 4 5 6 7 8 9 0 PIP 1 9 8 7 6 5 4 3 2 1

ISBN: 978-0-87051-972-7

Publisher: Amy M. Plent
Senior Managing Editor: Amy Krasnyanskaya
Acquisitions Editor: Erin Valentine

# Preface

## The Trend

### Contractor Nation

DRAMATIC AND PERMANENT MOVE TO CONTRACTING

> **"The demand for e-consultants is staggering. Technology consultants are commanding very large dollars."**
>
> ***Business Finance Magazine***

An estimated 30 million Americans are now working as part-time contractors, according to the Seattle Times (November 21, 2010). Each day, more of the work that gets done in business and other areas is being accomplished by employees who are contractors paid by the hour or project instead of regular full-time employees with a reliable paycheck.

Executives and professionals now make up around 10 percent of the temporary workforce.

HISTORY OF THE HIRED GUN ROLE

The bell curve in figure 1 demonstrates the demand for contract controllers and financial executives.

The position started to take shape in the early 1980s. By 1992, the demand for that role had grown tremendously in just 10 years. From 1990 to today the market has again expanded exponentially.

No one can say exactly how high the curve will go, but I suspect that there will always be a demand for the contract financial executive.

*The good news for you is that if you are considering this as a career choice there is unlimited potential.*

The good news for you if you are already serving as a hired gun is that there will always be a need for your services.

**Figure 1: Demand for Contract Controllers**

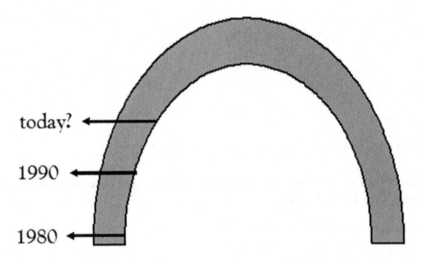

today? ←

1990 ←

1980 ←

## *Objectives*

You have the opportunity to provide top quality services at affordable prices without the human resource issues involved with having employees.

This fast-growing trend in business—requesting the services of a Financial Executive who is not a permanent part of the organization—means that for a variety of reasons, some companies are opting to

- Employ a person who works less than full-time.

- Staff a major project with temporary employees.

- Contract with an employee from their CPA advisory firm.

- Contract with a highly experienced Controller or CFO for an indefinite but short-term period of time.

This trend raises many questions, problems, and opportunities.

This book is designed to provide answers and guidance to many of the questions raised with this novel situation. Despite the unique need for Controllers, there is not much practical information on the subject.

After reading this book you should be able to

- Apply the special skills required of the part-time and contract Controller.

- Understand the role the contract Controller plays.

- Weigh the positives and negatives of being a part-time and contract Controller.

- Know how to be a very effective contract Controller.

- Discuss issues related to the elusive contract executive position.

- Develop a Position Description for a contract financial executive.

- Generate ideas on how to market yourself as a part-time or contract Controller.

- Design a tailored action plan for your specific needs.

- List your own ideas and contributions.

- Put this information to good use in your own career.

This book is designed for CFOs, Controllers, and anyone who chooses to work in a part-time or contract capacity. The specific duties are not as important as the attitudes and skill set. I will assume that you already know how to do accounting, so we will not cover number crunching. We will cover topics such as how you market yourself and how to deal with the ego-centric CEO.

## Assess Your Contract Professional Skill Set

| Self-Assessment #1: Where Do You Rate? | | | | | | | | |
|---|---|---|---|---|---|---|---|---|
| Be truly honest and rate your ability in each of these skill areas. If you are confused about the skill, read the explanation on the following pages. | | | | | | | | |
| | I Need to Work On | | | I Am Highly Skilled | | | | |
| Contract Professional Skill | Enter your score in the last column for each skill | | | | | | | My Score |
| Active Listening | 1 | 2 | 3 | 4 | 5 | 6 | 7 | 8 |
| Objective Observing | 1 | 2 | 3 | 4 | 5 | 6 | 7 | 8 |
| Objectivity and Clarity | 1 | 2 | 3 | 4 | 5 | 6 | 7 | 8 |
| Building Trust | 1 | 2 | 3 | 4 | 5 | 6 | 7 | 8 |
| Testing Assumptions | 1 | 2 | 3 | 4 | 5 | 6 | 7 | 8 |
| Partnering | 1 | 2 | 3 | 4 | 5 | 6 | 7 | 8 |
| Problem Solving | 1 | 2 | 3 | 4 | 5 | 6 | 7 | 8 |
| Integrative Thinking | 1 | 2 | 3 | 4 | 5 | 6 | 7 | 8 |
| Selling Ideas | 1 | 2 | 3 | 4 | 5 | 6 | 7 | 8 |
| Professionalism | 1 | 2 | 3 | 4 | 5 | 6 | 7 | 8 |
| Taking a Firm Stance | 1 | 2 | 3 | 4 | 5 | 6 | 7 | 8 |
| Total Score | 1 | 2 | 3 | 4 | 5 | 6 | 7 | 8 |

*(continued)*

**Answer Key**

*Scores of 77 to 88*

Wow! If you are not doing it now, you are ready to be a contract professional! Your next steps are to coach and mentor others so they can develop these skills too, while building up your practice.

*Scores of 66 to 76*

You are utilizing your skills well! You are very close to being ready to be a successful contractor, so your next steps are to seek out opportunities where you can increase the skills you scored lowest on and obtain honest feedback from the people you work with.

*Scores of 55 to 64*

You are contributing and make differences in small ways! However there are larger issues that you need to address. Your next step is to focus on the skills that you rated lowest on and seek out opportunities to practice those skills over and over until you have mastered them.

*Scores of 44 to 54*

You are only halfway to being considered an effective Controller and contract professional. The next steps you must take are to raise the bar for yourself and consider getting a mentor who will teach you the skills that you lack and challenge you to become more of who you can be.

*Scores Below 44*

Ouch! You either took the wrong class because you are not ready or are thinking that you are more effective than results show. You have a clear choice: 1) reevaluate your career choice, or 2) find ways to get out from behind your desk and become a more proactive agent of change each day, both inside your company and in volunteer situations. Failure to do this will cause harm to your earning potential. Sorry!

**Answer This Question:**

What did you learn about yourself as a contract financial executive?

*Contract Professional Skills Explained*

The following are a list of skills, along with descriptions of those skills, that are necessary for the successful contract professional.

ACTIVE LISTENING

- 100 percent of your being is involved when you are actively listening!

- Hearing is a physiological reaction, while listening is a mental process.

- Hearing is automatic, while listening is a conscious choice.

- Listening cannot be substituted by another skill.

- Over 40 percent of communication is the process of listening.

## OBJECTIVE OBSERVING

- Sitting back without an emotional attachment to what is in front of you and seeing it as a child would.

- Observing or watching to see the entire picture and the parts that are not readily evident.

## OBJECTIVITY

- Staying above the problem or issue.

- Not taking sides.

## CLARITY

- Seeing the event or issue with fresh eyes.

- Using your entire thinking abilities to see things clearly for insights and undiscovered truths.

## BUILDING TRUST

- Inspiring in others their confidence in your ability and character.

- Making others feel assured that you will not cause harm.

## TESTING ASSUMPTIONS

- The ability to analyze your or other people's assumptions surrounding an issue to identify and remove any biases.

- Working to remove any paradigms that you use to filter out information that conflicts with your deeply-rooted beliefs.

## PARTNERING

- Thinking and behaving collaboratively.

- Keeping the client's best interests in everything you do.

## PROBLEM SOLVING

- Looking for solutions that not only stop the problem today but help to prevent it from occurring again tomorrow.

- Using a wide variety of tools and insights to get to the core of the problem, while not getting bogged down with the side issues.

## INTEGRATIVE THINKING

- The use of facilitation tools to develop tailored and thoughtful recommendations for any unique situation.

- Learning quickly as time passes, using a variety of methodology.

## SELLING IDEAS

- Being able to convince or persuade someone with your arguments and logic.

- Selling ideas runs the gamut from simply stating the obvious to negotiating with another person.

## PROFESSIONALISM

- The expectation that a person will act as an expert at a reliable level of integrity.

- Competence and integrity are essential to professionalism.

## TAKING A FIRM STANCE

- Living up to your role as the conscience of your firm. There will be times when you have to take a firm stand against something that nearly everyone else believes is a good choice.

- The Controller needs to be able to clearly state their convictions and use that stance to persuade others.

# Contents

**Chapter 4: Attitudes for Success**

**Chapter 5: How Can I Ensure I Will Be Successful?**

## Chapter 6: Hired Gun Skills—Part 1

## Chapter 7: Hired Gun Skills—Part 2

# Chapter 1
# Controller Responsibilities

## Introduction

What is a Controller? Do they really control anything?

To fully understand the role of the contract controller, we need to set a baseline of knowledge about what the controller position is all about. This position is different from the CFO, which is covered in chapter 2.

This chapter helps you to

- Understand the role the Controller plays in an organization.

- Avoid getting sucked into the Controller's Vacuum.

- Help another professional decide if the role is one they really want to get involved with.

## The Controller Position

An experienced Controller described his job as:

> **"Do everything!"**

A seasoned Controller commented that her entire job description reads:

> **"All duties as assigned."**

The best way for a non-Controller to understand what a Controller does is to hear how many Controllers describe their job:

> **"A Controller has full responsibility for everything not specifically assigned to other executives."**

We begin understanding the contract Controller position by conducting a brief review of the Controller position. This is for two reasons. First, some people who are interested in this position come from public accounting and most have never served as Controller. This brief review gives them a better understanding of what responsibilities the Controller takes on so they can successfully scope out the client's project.

The second reason for this review is for people working in industry who have never been a Controller but are considering becoming a contractor. They want and need to know which responsibilities to accept and which to avoid.

The biggest understanding you will get from this review is being able to avoid getting sucked into the Controller's Vacuum.

> **Activity 1-1: Perils of Pauline, Part 1**
>
> Your good friend, Pauline, is asked to be the contract Controller in a critical position where the retiring incumbent averaged 55 hours per week. You know that she does not want to work that many hours.
>
> **Discussion Question**
>
> As her friend and mentor, what would you want to discuss with Pauline? Prepare an agenda of items to discuss and questions to ask her.

## *Avoid the Controller's Vacuum*

The Controller's Vacuum, a term that I coined to describe this phenomenon, is something that the Hired Gun must avoid at all costs. If you get sucked into this vacuum, I guarantee you will not be successful in the role as a contract professional. The vacuum is depicted in figure 1–1.

**Figure 1-1: How Our Responsibilities Grow**

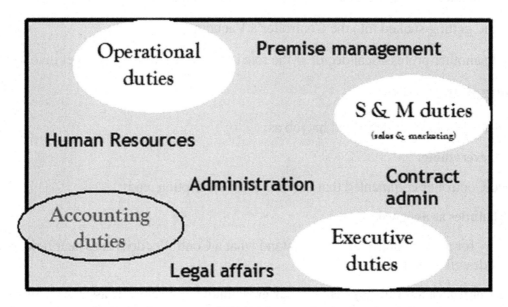

Figure 1-1 represents all the major responsibilities in a typical organization. There are normally specific executives responsible for marketing, production, and sales. You are hired to take over the traditional accounting duties—cash management, receivables, payables, payroll, internal controls, bank relations, and debt management.

But then:

"Since you handle payroll could you also take care of our human resource issues? We do not have anyone supervising the administrative personnel so could you take this on? Will you work with the attorneys on this complex legal issue? Could you make sure that we are in compliance with these government contracts? Employees are worried about building security. Would you look into it? Would you please handle the move to our new location since I do not have the time?"

Because you care and you have the expertise, you say "yes" to each of these requests. You just got sucked into the Controller's Vacuum! We quickly fill in all the shaded responsibilities.

Controllers traditionally end up being responsible for everything else not specifically assigned to other managers. Some Controllers manage all or part of operational areas in addition to the traditional finance and administration duties.

Now this is not true in large corporations, but you will not be hired as a contract Controller for Microsoft or IBM. The need for this role is in smaller companies that have executive or management teams of less than ten people.

The extensive responsibility borne by today's Controller creates a major problem for the contract or part-time Controller. Most Controllers work more than 50 hours every week and rarely achieve the feeling of "being caught up."

Therefore, you must avoid being asked to take on the entire workload borne by the full-time incumbent Controller. You can do so by understanding exactly what the client needs then agreeing only to fill that specific role or need. Later in this book, you will be given a tool titled the Position Description (exhibit 5-1), which will help you identify the proper role that matches the client's need to your expertise.

## The Role of the Controller

A good place to start is to define the niche the Controller fills in most organizations.

| **Answer This Question** |
| --- |
| What major roles do Controllers normally take on? |

### *Major Roles of a High Road Controller*

The major roles of a Controller include

- Being the internal financial consultant.

- Serving as the conscience for business ethics.

- Ensuring the control system works.

- Informing the employees, executives, and owners on how the company is doing financially.

- Keeping interested third parties supplied with adequate information.

- Being the main contact with bankers, investors, advisors, and government agencies.

- Adding value by making overhead functions cost effective and fully supportive, while ensuring efficiency in the supply chain.

- Being a positive role model and forceful leader.

- Providing insight and suggest courses of action.

In the next chapter, the role of the Controller is compared and contrasted against the role of the CFO.

## BE THE INTERNAL FINANCIAL CONSULTANT

People within the organization look to you as their primary resource. They are always turning to you to get questions answered and problems solved. We love to do this; yet it is a very time consuming and open-ended responsibility.

## SERVE AS THE CONSCIENCE FOR BUSINESS ETHICS

In addition to being responsible for the internal controls, the Controller or CFO is the conscience of the organization. You must ensure that people are acting ethically and that both the internal and external messages are clear about where the leaders stand on the issue of ethical conduct.

## ENSURE THE CONTROL SYSTEM WORKS

If it were not for the Controller this responsibility would never be taken on. It is one of the most important and most often minimized responsibilities.

## INFORM THE EMPLOYEES, EXECUTIVES, AND OWNERS AS TO HOW THE COMPANY IS DOING FINANCIALLY

Besides financial reporting, the Controller does a lot of communicating regarding goals, accomplishments, and problems. Since many of these have a financial impact, people want to know immediately what the impact will be. They turn to you for answers and predictions.

## KEEP INTERESTED THIRD PARTIES SUPPLIED WITH ADEQUATE INFORMATION

The Controller is usually the one who provides information to third parties besides the bank and government agencies. Vendors, customers, and others who have a stake in the business's success want to know what is going on.

## BE THE MAIN CONTACT WITH BANKERS, INVESTORS, ADVISORS, AND GOVERNMENT AGENCIES

As the Controller, you are usually the main contact with these organizations and professionals. Even if you are not the main contact, you usually supervise the person who is.

## ADD VALUE BY MAKING OVERHEAD FUNCTIONS COST EFFECTIVE AND FULLY SUPPORTIVE, WHILE ENSURING EFFICIENCY IN THE SUPPLY CHAIN

As you are well aware, accounting is much more than counting beans. The accounting team must be a profit center by adding value such as looking for cost savings and identifying unexploited opportunities for profits or revenues. Ensuring the efficiency of their organization's supply chain is a growing area where Controllers are heavily involved.

BE A POSITIVE ROLE MODEL AND FORCEFUL LEADER

First and foremost, the Controller and the CFO are forceful leaders in their organizations. Employees at all levels look to you as a role model and pay particular attention to what you do, what you say, and how you act when you think no one is watching.

PROVIDE INSIGHT AND SUGGEST COURSES OF ACTION

Finally, because of our insight into how the organization functions from an inside-out view, we are in the prime position to offer specific courses of action. This insight into what is going well and what is not can help the organization's leaders to be more effective. This is one of the most exciting responsibilities of the Controller or CFO and yet one of the most overlooked and ignored.

## The Controller's Major Responsibilities

Without looking at specific Controller job descriptions, we can understand the major responsibilities of the job by dissecting the various functions of a typical business organization, as illustrated in exhibit 1-1.

**Exhibit 1-1: Organizational Functions of a Typical Business**

**Organizational Functions of a Typical Business**

| Product/Service Sales | Operations |
|---|---|
| □ marketing and advertising | □ product/service R and D |
| □ sales | □ product/service production |
| □ customer service | □ product/service delivery |
| □ product pricing | □ product/service support |
| □ customer retention | □ product facilities management |
| **Management** | **Administration** |
| □ executive policy or decision-making | □ support services |
| □ mergers or acquisitions | □ record retention |
| □ strategic planning | □ facilities management and security |
| □ short-term planning | □ purchasing |
| □ budgeting | □ communications and training |
| □ project implementation | □ human resources |
| **Finance** | **Information Systems** |
| □ general accounting | □ computer systems |
| □ credit and collections | □ telecommunication systems |
| □ billing | □ user support |
| □ external reporting | □ maintenance and repairs |
| □ internal reporting | □ future system development |
| □ treasury management | |

---

**Self-Assessment #2: What Is Your Sleep Number?**

Use exhibit 1-1 to check [√] all the organizational functions that you believe a Controller should have primary responsibility for. If you are currently a Controller, check all that you are responsible for.

How many functions did you check? _____ (Out of 33 possible)

---

---

**Activity 1-2: Perils of Pauline, Part 2**

As you meet with Pauline to help her understand the role of the contract Controller, you show her the previous list of responsibilities. She only wants to work 25 to 30 hours per week as a Controller. She asks to address these:

**Discussion Questions**

What will be her difficulty in assigning a priority hierarchy to the responsibilities you checked?

How would you go about doing this so she can follow your lead?

---

## Conclusion

The organization's Controller has a wide variety of responsibilities, some of them are accounting related and others are not. If you ignore the Controller's Vacuum you could quickly find yourself with too many responsibilities. While this might help in job security, it is not an ideal condition for contract Controllers.

As you go about deciding if you want to be a contract Controller or want to continue as one, you must understand the full spectrum of responsibilities that Controllers and their team take on. This understanding will help you to define your role when you put yourself on the market as a contractor.

**Job permanence for the Controller is becoming less common.**

Whether you serve as full-time, part-time, or contract controller, you must make a personal commitment to stay on the ethical High Road, because you will be tested.

# Chapter 2
# CFO Responsibilities

**"The CFO must be the one asking questions that others are reluctant to ask. He must be the one others regard as the person without an agenda."**

## Introduction

For the person who wants to consult at a high level, while having significant impact, being a contract CFO is the ultimate head rush. Since 1992, the men and women I met who serve as a contract CFO tell me that they love their job. The three things they enjoy most are

- The high level at which they get to work.

- The tremendous impact they have on their clients.

- The high fees they earn.

Hired Gun CFOs tell me that their clients rarely question the amount of the fee. In fact, their clients tend to rely on their advice and counsel so much that their engagements continue for years.

This chapter will highlight just a few of the nuances that will enable the contract CFO to function at the strategic level.

Completion of this chapter will allow you to

- Understand the high-level role that the contract CFO is asked to undertake.

- Apply the critical skills that a contract CFO will need to be strategic.

- Contrast how the CFO's role differs from that of the Controller.

- Use the Economic Value Added reporting tool to help the client manage both profits and balance sheet investments.

## Attributes of the CFO

> Mike McCracken, President of Tatum CFO Partners, an Atlanta based firm that provides clients with CFO talent on a short-term basis, said this in an interview in *Business Finance Magazine*.
>
> "CFOs are not likely to have a career with one company and stay there."
>
> "You need expertise in areas like finance and accounting and capital markets, but adaptability is the most important [mindset]."

> **Answer This Question**
>
> What is it like to operate at the strategic level? How would it differ from being a day-to-day Controller?

A member of our esteemed profession, Joseph Ripp, CFO of Time Warner said in a speech: "The CFO must be the one asking questions that others are reluctant to ask. He must be the one others regard as the person without an agenda." By extension, his message also applies to the Controller.

In response to the question above, my answer would be that leading at the strategic level requires the CFO to be the true conscience of the firm. You must be the person who is willing to raise issues and counsel other leaders on the viability of their goals, plans, and policies. You must be seen as the professional leader who does not have any biases or an agenda other than the success of the organization.

Amazingly, all the attributes that you rely on to mentor an individual are the same ones you use in being a CFO. You must still be able to listen beyond the words, use questions to open up dialogue, build trust between yourself and your colleagues, and ultimately guide people's thinking and behaviors. Let us recap those attributes.

## *Teaching and Training*

As the CFO, you are constantly teaching others about the nuances of finance, accounting, and business management. Your position is moving toward that of a constant trainer.

## *Counseling*

You will need to hold the hands of other leaders and colleagues as you guide them through difficult situations and tough decisions. In leading at the strategic level, you will often act as a counselor who dispenses advice and suggestions. You will often need to dispense tough love as well. Sorry, this responsibility comes with the job of being the conscience of your organization.

## *Guiding*

Just as in mentoring an individual, you must guide the actions and decisions of other leaders in terms of making ethical choices, relying on checks and balances, and wise decisions. While it would be nice if every leader in your organization had integrity, meaning that they walk their talk each day, you know this is not always the case. Once you choose to be the Controller or CFO, you must be willing to shape other leaders' behaviors and decisions so that they stay focused on plans and solutions that benefit the customer, the organization, and ultimately the shareholders instead of themselves.

## *Learning*

Although you are an accomplished professional, you still have many things to learn. By keeping an open mind and knowing that you can learn from the examples of other members of the leadership team, you will ensure your future success and discover that there are many other avenues to channel your talents in the organization. Over the years, I have met CFOs who used their experiences and knowledge to become CEOs, venture capitalists, hedge fund managers, niche consultants, and operations executives. The CFO's job is a launching pad that opens up to the unlimited opportunities available to the person who is willing to stretch beyond what is comfortable and predictable.

## Sharing

Just as in mentoring an individual, you will be sharing your insights and wisdom with others in the form of stories, examples, and analogies. This is why this workshop requires you to spend most of the day sharing your story.

## Questioning

One of the more powerful tools a CFO uses is thoughtful questioning. Instead of relying on declarative statements, a good leader uses questions to open people's eyes and minds to new possibilities. Very often executives and managers are so focused on their issues or goals that they get bogged down in their personal agendas. Because of your wisdom and experiences, you see clearly what the leadership team needs to do to achieve and accomplish its strategic initiatives. Therefore, to be an effective CFO you must get in the habit of using questions—open-ended and pointed—to get the leadership team to create the conclusions that will help them get to where the organization needs to go.

## Relating

One of the strongest ways that you, the CFO, builds bridges and fosters relationships of trust is to use analogies, examples, and stories to get your point across. This means you must speak at the same level of the person you are talking to. The CFO will use examples and stories from many different sources. This requires you to constantly be listening, learning, and growing.

## Listening

Along with the skill of questioning, as the organization's internal leader, you will rely intensively on the ability to listen with your ears as well as your eyes and intuition. Managers with hidden agendas or hubris will rarely speak clearly and address the issue. Instead they will circle around the issue. They will resist. They will deny anything is wrong. Your job is to listen to what is said and unsaid in order to get a sense of what the person is not saying or trying to hide. By listening carefully and using questions, you become more of the conscience by bringing forth those things that need to be expressed and brought out into the open.

## Intuitiveness

Just as in mentoring the individual, over time you will develop a keen sense of what to say and not to say. We call this business sense, but it is in fact your intuitiveness. It is wisdom you hone from your experiences both within the organization and from without. This is why some executive teams only want a CFO or Controller with gray hair because they feel, with age, this person has developed a strong sense of what to do. While I disagree with this practice, it is human nature for us to assume that only people of a certain age have become in touch with their intuitiveness.

Remember that your intuitiveness is both an asset and your ally to be an effective CFO.

## *Creativity*

The creativity that the CFO needs to be successful in getting others to change is one of being open-minded to new possibilities. This skill works hand-in-hand with your intuitiveness. Your creativity comes into fruition when you think of tools, methods, or processes that the organization and other leaders can use to remove obstacles that hinder execution of the plans.

Therefore, as CFO it is incumbent on you to be constantly thinking of tools and best practices that the leadership team can use to make progress toward the corporate goals and strategic initiatives.

## How the CFO and Controller's Roles Differ

The CFO and the Controller are intimately involved in meeting the organization's fiscal or financial goals and objectives. The responsibilities of the Chief Financial Officer are broader and extend far beyond the finance department.

Typically more externally oriented, a CFO is concerned with organization-wide and marketplace issues. As an executive with a deep understanding of finance, as well as broad-based business knowledge, who serves on the leadership team, the CFO is responsible for bringing the financial point of view to the forefront in their organization's most crucial decisions. The board and owners (shareholders or members) look to their CFO to establish, maintain, and monitor the vital Governance Program.

The Controller is generally more narrowly focused on the issues and obligations of the finance department, administration areas, and, most critically, the internal control structure. While the Controller's responsibilities may be less broad than those of a CFO, a good Controller must be prepared to back up their CFO. A wise Controller will develop a deep understanding of how their organization works and will provide the necessary skills that support their CFO's responsibilities.

Both financial professionals must be viewed as a business partner and, therefore, take a proactive role by participating in both management and operational decision-making.

As you will see in table 2-1, the CFO and Controller positions can be seen as quite different in their scope and orientation. It is unwise to assume that someone with Controller experience can automatically move into the role of the CFO, or that someone who has been a CFO is also excellent at the responsibilities of the Controller. Some organizations prefer a CFO who is not a CPA to ensure that he or she lacks a "bean counter" mentality. A good CFO must avoid having a "green eye-shade" mentality.

## *Responsibility Comparison*

Table 2-1 shows the overall responsibilities of the two key roles. Notice that the CFO must take ownership for global and firm-wide issues while the Controller must take ownership for the accounting team and its impact on finances and service.

**Table 2-1: CFO and Controller Responsibility Comparison**

| Scope of Responsibility | CFO | Controller[*] |
|---|---|---|
| Have Concern for the Marketplace | Very important | Important |
| Have a Global Organizational Awareness | Very important | Important |
| Have a Board Orientation | Very important | Important |
| Be the Management Team Builder | Very important | Important |
| Be the Fiscal Policy-Setter | Very important | Important |
| Implement the Governance Program | Very important | Important |
| Be the Strategist | Very important | Important |
| Be the Change Agent | Very important | Very important |
| Communication Nexus | Very important | Very important |
| Be the Firm's Conscience | Very important | Very important |
| Instill an Attitude of Service in Finance | Very important | Very important |
| Establish the Culture | Very important | Important |
| Be the Financial Policy Setter | Important | Important |
| Finance Team Builder | Important | Very important |
| Be the Efficiency Expert | Less important | Very important |
| Be the GAAP Expert | Less important | Very important |
| Know Each Team Member's Effectiveness | Less important | Very important |
| Be the Work Organizer | Less important | Very important |

[*] This comparison assumes that the Controller reports to a CFO. If the leader of the finance function, especially in a small organization, serves as both Controller and CFO, then many of the responsibilities designated for a CFO must be assumed by the Controller.

## Functional Role Comparison

The roles of the CFO and Controller must complement each other, with each person bringing his or her unique skill set to the table so that together they serve to fulfill an essential organizational function, what we refer to in the encompassing term "Accounting."

Basically, the CFO's functional role is to help define the big picture and develop or assist in developing global strategies that carry out the organization's mission. The Controller then uses his or her resources and technical knowledge to execute those strategies with specific tactics. Through the Controller's reporting responsibility, the executive team will obtain timely feedback regarding their strategy's viability and on employees' efforts to carry out the designated tactics.

While both serve as a vital communication nexus, the CFO essentially fulfills the role as the main interface between the finance function and the board or executive team and between the finance function and the shareholders. On the other hand, a Controller is the main interface between the finance function and all internal departments, and between the finance function and most external stakeholders (IRS, vendors, et al.). Table 2-2 compares the roles of the CFO and the Controller in each major functional area.

**Table 2-2: CFO and Controller Functional Role Comparison**

| Major Functional Area | CFO's Role | Controller's Role* |
|---|---|---|
| Financial Reporting (external feedback) | Identifies external reporting needs; presents and explains financial reports. | Prepares external financial reports. |
| Management Reporting (internal feedback) | Develops framework on ways and means for reporting; provides a common focus on Key Performance Indicators that measure the firm's strategy. | Develops appropriate reporting structure; prepares reports and weds financial and non-financial data; provides a monthly State of the Union. |
| Treasury Management | Develops overall treasury strategy in line with operational and capital plans; maintains ongoing and open relationships with investors and bankers. | Monitors and supervises asset balances, investments, borrowings, and fund transfers. |
| Risk Management | Assesses exposure and calculates firm's risk tolerance; determines insurance coverage requirements. | Administers insurance portfolio; provides risk assessment tools to employees. |
| Budgeting | Establishes broad budget parameters based on the Strategic Plan; presents budget to board and executive council for review and approval. | Facilitates the budget process; aids in the development of detailed budgets based upon Operating Plan; monitors overall budget. |
| Strategic Planning | Sponsors or manages the annual planning retreat; represents finance's interests in plans; presents overall financial picture to board and executive council. | Prepares analyses and information to be used by retreat participants. |
| Performance Analysis | Identifies operational and financial areas to be measured; establishes success factors; establishes firm-wide scorecard; reviews actual performance against targets with board and executive council. | Designs, prepares, and distributes operational, financial, statistical, and other reports that measure actual performance against targets. |

*This comparison assumes that the Controller reports to a CFO. If the leader of the finance function, especially in a small organization, serves as both Controller and CFO, then many of the roles designated for a CFO may fall to the Controller.

# CFO Tool: Calculating the Economic Value Added

A specific area where the CFO can help their employer or client is to determine if they are truly making a profit. Many small businesses go under because, on paper, the business was profitable but not returning the net cash flow necessary to cover the cost of capital. This strategic thinking tool, called the Economic Value Added is something the contract CFO can use to immediately help a client determine their true profitability picture.

## *Economic Value Added Defined*

Economic Value Added (EVA) is a decision-making tool to determine if an investment of capital is generating a return. It is a measurement of the business unit's cash contribution after removing what could have been earned elsewhere.

Economic Value Added objectively helps

- Evaluate a business unit's performance.

- Reward teams for performance.

- Plan strategically.

*EVA assumes that capital is not free.* This is very important! Owners and managers are mindful of how much debt costs because of the interest rate. They also believe that the capital contributions from stock purchases are free because there is no interest rate applied to them.

Since every operating business unit consumes capital of some kind, the manager of each unit must understand that the more capital they need to operate, the more profit they must generate to cover the cost of the capital. This is determined as the opportunity cost of capital.

A typical operating unit consumes capital through these five balance sheet items:

- Accounts receivable

- Inventory

- Depreciable assets

- Amortizable assets

- Non-depreciable assets

Assume that there is a business unit that sells its products for cash, carries no inventory, and does not require any fixed assets to operate. Intuitively we know that this is both an efficient operation and a highly profitable one.

Assume that there is a business unit that ties up millions of dollars in receivables, inventory, and depreciable assets. Oh, and its margins are razor thin! Intuitively we know that the margins are not covering the cost of capital we invest in the unit. That is the basis for the EVA—charging each operating unit for the cost of the capital it needs to operate.

EVA FORMULA

> After tax cash flows – opportunity cost of capital = Economic Value Added

CALCULATION OF EVA IN FOUR STEPS

*Step 1*

Determine (isolate) the business unit to be analyzed—this includes isolating and assigning its share of inventory, receivables, and debt.

*Step 2*

Calculate income before interest and after income taxes—this removes the effect of debt interest on profits.

*Step 3*

Calculate the total capital employed in the business unit—this includes long-term debt, shareholders' equity, preferred stock, and other capital contributions.

*Step 4*

Determine the opportunity cost of capital—this is the rate the company would have paid for primary capital in the open market.

REPORTING THE ECONOMIC VALUE ADDED

Please see example 2-1 for an example of one of these reports.

*What to Do Next*

After the EVA is calculated it needs to be evaluated. Something needs to be done, hopefully to increase the recovery of your cost of capital. This is where the CFO helps the client decide what to do with this insightful information.

*EVA Decision Alternatives*

Eva decision alternatives include the following:

- Do nothing.

- Invest more capital.

- Improve or streamline operations.

- Replace management.

- Divest the unit.

- Liquidate the unit.

**Example 2-1**

| Raelco Industries<br>EVA Calculation for 2008 | Per<br>books | EVA<br>adjustment | | EVA<br>calculation |
|---|---|---|---|---|
| Operating profits | 50,000 | | | 50,000 |
| Interest expense | 10,000 | [1] | (10,000) | 0 |
| Pretax profit | 40,000 | | 10,000 | 50,000 |
| Income tax (40 percent) | 16,000 | [2] | 4,000 | 20,000 |
| Net income after taxes (NIAT) | 24,000 | | 6,000 | 30,000 |
| | | | | |
| [3] Debt at 15 percent cost | 50,000 | | | 50,000 |
| [4] Shareholders equity at 11 percent cost | 80,000 | | | 80,000 |
| [5] Preferred Stock cost at 18 percent cost | 20,000 | | | 20,000 |
| Total capitalization | 150,000 | | | 150,000 |
| [6] Blended cost of capital per annum | | | | × 13.2 percent |
| Opportunity cost of capital | | | | 19,800 |
| | | | | |
| Cash flows contribution (NIAT) | | | | **30,000** |
| Less: Opportunity cost of capital | | | | **(19,800)** |
| | | | | |
| **Economic Value Added** | | | | **$ 10,200** |

Notes and explanations:

[1] Interest expense is removed from operating profits because it will be added back later based upon how much capital the operating unit consumes.

[2] Since deductible interest expense has been removed, the impact on income tax must also be adjusted.

[3] Use the actual interest rate paid or calculate an average if you have multiple rates. Use the actual rates that applied during the operating profit period.

[4] This will be your toughest calculation. You must assign an interest rate that represents the return that non-preferred shareholders would expect if you compensated them for their capital. This figure often represents how much they theoretically could receive if they have invested their money in another less risky investment. You should not assume a rate such as a bank CD, because the risk-taking entrepreneur would select something more risky such as real estate or discounted bonds.

[5] Use a rate that would approximate the amount of return given to the preferred shareholders, either in cash or appreciation. One way to evaluate this is to ask: "How much interest would we pay them if the preferred shareholder loaned us this money?"

[6] If you are a spreadsheet wizard, calculate a blended or weighted average of the debt, preferred, and capital return rates. Make sure this blended rate is reasonable and truly represents the mix of all sources of long-term capital. If you use long-term leases to have a clean balance sheet, you will need to factor those in as well.

## WAYS TO MAKE EVA MEANINGFUL

Ways to make EVA meaningful include the following:

- Help the company's leaders calculate their EVA for each business unit.

- Offer to design a simplified method to determine the EVA for each major investment of capital.

- Help employees discover how their day-to-day decisions impact the EVA.

- Be a facilitator for the leadership team on what the next steps might be once the EVA is determined and evaluated.

**Box 2-1: Comparison of Economic Value Added to the Balanced Scorecard**

| <u>Balanced Scorecard</u> | <u>Economic Value Added</u> |
|---|---|

| Objectives: |
|---|
| Enhancing profitability by focusing on major areas beyond financial measures. |
| Allowing managers to plan strategically for specific areas and translate their goals into measurable outcomes. |

| Objectives: |
|---|
| Increasing shareholder value where the management and shareholders are tied together via stock ownership. |
| Focusing managers to look at the long-term economic return on their business decisions. |

| Focus: |
|---|
| Aligned and balanced measures. |
| Four specific areas: learning and growth; internal process; customer; financial. |
| Balance of long-term and short-term. |

| Focus: |
|---|
| True cost of all capital employed. |
| Profits after deducting capital employed. |
| Valuing all capital employed in the business. |
| Reducing the capital used to a minimum. |

| Process: |
|---|
| Ties strategy to metrics. |
| Uses internal measures. |
| Uses benchmarking. |

| Process: |
|---|
| Ties metrics to value creation. |
| Uses internal and external metrics. |
| Uses stock price or cost of capital. |

| Minimum Requirements: |
|---|
| Visionary leadership |
| Culture that supports planning |
| Aligned metrics |
| Alignment vertically and horizontally |
| Excellent IT system |
| Rewards and incentives |
| Ability to react quickly |

| Minimum Requirements: |
|---|
| Visionary leadership |
| Culture that supports planning |
| Aligned metrics |
| Cost of capital definition |
| Excellent IT system |
| Rewards and incentives |
| Ability to focus on the long-term |

| Incentives: | Incentives: |
|---|---|
| Solely based upon the balanced metrics, usually capped | Based on the EVA, increases without caps or limits |

| Source: | Source: |
|---|---|
| David Norton and Robert Kaplan | Stern Stewart and Co. |

## Conclusion

Job permanence of the CFO is becoming a thing of the past.

In a large firm, the CFO is a strategic partner of the CEO and provides global guidance on the appropriate path to take for the organization. In a smaller firm, the CFO is the strategic partner of the owners and provides global guidance. The difference is that in the smaller firm the CFO is the person who actually gets to implement part or the entire strategic path. The small company CFO is in a unique position to see the whole picture, yet roll up their sleeves to tinker with the organization to make it better.

The CFO uses a variety of attributes such as those listed in this chapter to help the organization and its leaders understand where they are going based upon where they have been. In this chapter, a CFO level tool—the Economic Value Added—is the sort of analysis that the CFO uses to conduct strategic decision-making.

Understanding this role will help you should you decide to be a contract CFO.

A good contract CFO has the ability to monitor the ever-changing landscape for business trends including best practices that work and ones that do not. This person has the ability to pull together firm-wide knowledge and overcome learning curves faster than the current staff.

# Chapter 3

# What Is the Contract Controller's Job About?

**It is not the contract that defines what you need to do!**

## Introduction

Now that we have summarized and differentiated the role of the Controller and of the CFO, let us get more specific about the job of the contractor or Hired Gun.

While there are a tremendous amount of similarities, there are some differences and the rest of the book will highlight them. Even if you decide that being a contractor or part-timer is not for you, you still will get tremendous value as we focus on the skills and attitudes that contribute to a Hired Gun's success.

For everyone who is currently or has been a Controller, your job description (I assume you had one...but you know the joke about making assumptions!) defines what you accepted responsibility for. As we delve into the role that the contract Controller plays, we will start with analyzing several job descriptions for actual Controllers.

After completing this chapter you should be able to

- Redefine the role you must play to benefit your client or employer.

- Decide which duties you will take responsibility for.

- Recognize the reasons why a company might need a contract Controller or CFO.

- Understand the general role the contract professional plays.

- Use the Controller's mantle of authority for positive results.

- Select a role that fits your interests.

## Main Difference in Expectation of the Roles

When you are hired as the Controller in a regular situation (meaning that you are a full-time employee and not under contract) your employer gives you time to learn the job. Under normal circumstances a newly hired Controller has about 6 months to master the job and learn the business. This window is less for a simple organization and longer for a complicated business model.

Now here is the thing that shocks most people when they first become a contract Controller, which discourages some of them from pursuing this as a viable career option:

**The learning curve for a contract Controller or CFO is two weeks!**

When you are brought in as a consultant, the client places extreme expectations on you to have an immediate impact. In fact, several experienced contract professionals have told me that their clients expected some sort of measurable results within the first week. This is a tremendous amount of pressure to be placed on anyone.

This is mentioned as a warning to those considering becoming a contract Controller or CFO. You need to understand this seemingly unreasonable demand from your clients.

As a Hired Gun you have billed yourself as an expert in solving accounting problems. Since you have sold yourself to the client as such, the client will, in turn, expect to see immediate results from your efforts.

---

**Answer This Question**

Can you learn the client's business and define your real role in two weeks?

---

**"The aftermath of the downsizing year coupled with today's tight job market often leaves managers unable to cope with additional assignments, especially major strategic initiatives. The company may lack sufficient internal talent to solve a problem."**

*Business Finance Magazine*

**Worldwide, consulting revenues top $100 billion per year with an annual 20 percent growth rate.**

## The Controller Job Description

Review the three job descriptions for real-life Controller positions on the following pages. They are all different, yet there are three commonalities among them.

- Many of the duties are the same (although described differently).

- The job of the Controller is very broad.

- The written description rarely covers all the duties of the Controller.

---

**Activity 3-1: Perils of Pauline, Part 3**

Pauline provides you a copy of the incumbent's job description (sample job description #3). The company President wants her to work at a high level and get quick results.

Go through the job duty section and mark out (X) or revise all the duties you think would not be appropriate for Pauline to accept as a contract Controller working less than full-time.

---

> **Answer This Question**
>
> Consider the choices you made in the above activity. Why did you make those particular choices? What did you learn?

## The Point of this Exercise

The Controller's Vacuum is a very real phenomenon and one that can undermine your effectiveness as a contract or part-time Controller. In this exercise, you were required to thoughtfully and carefully analyze the responsibilities against the objective of working at a high level.

As you quickly discovered, many of the duties or responsibilities needed revision. Most of your improvements were to get Pauline out of the daily hands-on responsibility and more focused on analysis, overview, and consultation.

Use your new awareness to develop your own Position Description for the type of engagements you are undertaking or plan to undertake.

## Actual Job Description #1

> **GGG Corporation**
> **Job Title:** Controller
> **Supervisor:** President
>
> **Major Responsibilities:**
>
> ☐ Manage credit and collections to ensure sufficient cash flow; develop and implement credit policies; create and maintain credit files and forms; perform credit checks and make determinations of creditworthiness; enforce terms of sale.
>
> ☐ Project cash flow and manage disbursements accordingly.
>
> ☐ Maintain appropriate relationships with key vendors.
>
> ☐ Manage personnel functions; maintain personnel files; manage multi-state payroll; administer benefits such as our 401(k), Flex Plan, EAP, medical, dental, and disability insurance plans.
>
> ☐ Ensure company is in compliance with all required tax filings (multi-state, city and federal, as well as benefit plans).
>
> ☐ Be aware of appropriate OSHA & WISHA [Washington state's job safety] regulations and ensure compliance.
>
> ☐ Monitor use of company software to protect against piracy.
>
> ☐ Be responsible for integrity of the balance sheet; prepare monthly in-house financial statements; communicate with outside accountant for annual review.
>
> ☐ Manage relationship with bank for line of credit and provide monthly and quarterly reports as required by loan covenants.
>
> ☐ Other duties as needed.

## Actual Job Description #2

**Job Title:** Controller       **Department:** Administration
**Supervisor:** President
**Job Relationships:** Supervises managers of Accounting, Credit, Information Systems, and Inventory Control

**Position Summary:**
Manage and coordinate the financial activities of the company. Monitor adherence to Raelco Company's policies and procedures. Monitor cash flow and coordinate to ensure that adequate funds are available to finance Raelco's business. Hire, train, evaluate, and discharge employees in accordance with personnel policies.

**Duties and Responsibilities:**

- Manage, supervise, and coordinate the accounting and control of company assets, liabilities, and financial transactions in accordance with accepted accounting principles.

- Coordinate the development and updating of accounting procedures and systems.

- Oversee the maintenance of tax records.

- Oversee the general operation of the credit area of the company. Approve the granting of larger credits and assist with the collection of more serious problem accounts.

- Analyze monthly results and advise the president of unusual trends and variations from the plan. Provide recommendations for any corrective actions deemed appropriate.

- Analyze capital expenditure requests and other proposals. Provide input and recommendations from a financial perspective.

- Coordinate with LAX (our parent company) to ensure that adequate funds are available to finance planned business activities.

- Prepare periodic financial reports for LAX and others, as required.

- Prepare annual and 3-year Business Plans. Monitor department and division accomplishments against the general strategies and goals outlined in the business plans.

- Keep abreast of economic conditions and similar factors germane to the Company's best financial interest. Recommend alternatives in company strategies when required by changes in economic conditions.

- Ensure that individuals' incentive plans are compatible with company goals and objectives.

- Hire, train, evaluate, promote, and discharge employees in accordance with personnel policies.

- Ensure compliance with company policies and affirmative action program.

- Perform other general managerial duties as assigned.

**Qualifications:**

**Education & Experience**

Bachelors Degree in Business Administration, with an emphasis in Accounting or Finance. CPA required. Minimum of 10 years experience in accounting. Credit and collection experience preferred. Previous management experience necessary. Proficient with computers.

**Knowledge, Skills & Abilities**

Possess extensive knowledge of generally accepted accounting principles, efficient accounting procedures, credit investigation procedures, collection techniques, and inventory control. Have the ability to plan and organize work requirements. Possess good oral and written communication skills. Possess good analytical skills, and the ability to reach sound conclusions. Develop, handle, and work with proprietary, private, and confidential information.

## Actual Job Description #3

**Controller Job Summary Part 1**

**Accounting Responsibilities**

1. Plans, organizes, directs, and controls the accounting and control function of the division, reports operational results, and provides chronological systems.

2. Coordinates and administers an adequate plan for the control of operations. Such a plan provides profit planning, sales forecasts, expense budgets, accounts receivable, cost standards and saving opportunities, and capital investing, together with the necessary controls and procedures to effectuate the plan.

3. Compares performance with operating plans and standards. Provides reports and interprets the results of operations to all levels of management. This includes the formulation of accounting policies, the preparation of financial statements and operating data, the coordination of systems and procedures, and special reports as required.

4. Forecasts short-range and long-range cash requirements and obligations as a basis for maintaining adequate funds.

5. Assures protection for the assets of the business through internal control, internal auditing, while ensuring proper insurance coverage.

6. Monitors credit and collection applications and approves terms above a predetermined dollar amount.

*(continued)*

7. Assists Marketing in establishing and maintaining product-pricing policies.

8. Provides other company units with related information required by them to carry out their assigned responsibilities.

9. Establishes and implements a sound operational and organizational plan in direct support of the business plan.

10. Keeps the President informed of the division's performance and provides advice on all financial matters.

11. Executes cash disbursements for payment of corporate and divisional expenditures in accordance with disbursement and policies.

12. Monitors inventory levels and advises management regarding variances to budget.

13. Develops and presents to the President matters requiring his or her decision.

14. Assumes other special activities and responsibilities as required.

**Controller Job Summary Part 2**

**Management Responsibilities**

1. Develops and recommends budget. Authorizes expenditures in accordance with budget. Approves budget and expenses of subordinates.

2. Develops short- and long-range operating objectives, organizational structure, and staffing requirements.

3. Assures that the duties, responsibilities, and authority of each job are clearly defined, effective, and communicated to incumbents.

4. Assures that management training and development needs are identified, and programs initiated.

5. Assures that qualified personnel are selected and that orientation and on-the-job training programs are conducted and effective.

6. Develops an adequate plan for backup and succession of management and other key personnel.

7. Monitors performance of direct reports. Provides prompt and objective coaching and counseling. Reviews direct reports and approves performance appraisals initiated by direct reports. Ensures that a MBO-based performance appraisal system is administered effectively. [MBO means Management by Objectives.]

8. Assures that a positive employee relations position is maintained. Ensures that the company's management principles, policies, and programs are consistently practiced. Approves effective personnel action initiated by direct reports.

9. Assures that effective communications are maintained within areas of responsibility. Where appropriate, informs employees as to plans and progress. Conducts employee discussion sessions at regular and frequent intervals.

10. Assures that the necessary coordination within the area of responsibility is taking place and that coordination of the assigned area with those of other company or corporate units is taking place. Resolves problems involving coordination.

11. Consults with all segments of management responsible for policy or action. Makes recommendations for improving the effectiveness of policy or practices.

12. Acts within scope of authority and consistent with company and corporate objectives, guidelines, policies, and practices.

13. Ensures optimum performance of the function. Recommends and implements techniques to improve productivity, increase efficiencies, cut costs, take advantage of opportunities, and maintain state-of-the-art practices.

14. Keeps abreast of current trends and practices in field of expertise.

15. Assumes other special activities and responsibilities from time to time as directed.

## The Chief Financial Officer Job Description

### General Definition

The Chief Financial Officer (CFO) provides both operational and programmatic support to the organization. The CFO supervises the finance unit and is the chief financial spokesperson for the organization. The CFO reports directly to the President or Chief Executive Officer (CEO) and directly assists the Chief Operating Officer (COO) on all strategic and tactical matters as they relate to budget management, cost benefit analysis, forecasting needs, and the securing of new funding.

### Essential Duties and Responsibilities

The CFO's essential duties and responsibilities include the following:

- Assist in performing all tasks necessary to achieve the organization's mission and help execute staff succession and growth plans.

- Train the Finance Unit and other staff on raising awareness and knowledge of financial management matters.

- Work with the President or CEO on the strategic vision, including fostering and cultivating stakeholder relationships on city, state, and national levels, as well as assisting in the development and negotiation of contracts.

- Participate in developing new business; specifically, assist the CEO and COO in identifying new funding opportunities, the drafting of prospective programmatic budgets, and determining cost effectiveness of prospective service delivery.

- Assess the benefits of all prospective contracts and advise the Executive Team on programmatic design and implementation matters.

- Ensure adequate controls are installed and that substantiating documentation is approved and available, such that all purchases may pass independent and governmental audits.

- Provide the COO with an operating budget. Work with the COO to ensure programmatic success through cost analysis support and compliance with all contractual and programmatic requirements. This includes 1) interpreting legislative and programmatic rules and regulations to ensure compliance with all federal, state, local, and contractual guidelines; 2) ensuring that all government regulations and requirements are disseminated to appropriate personnel; and 3) monitoring compliance.

- Oversee the management and coordination of all fiscal reporting activities for the organization, including organizational revenue or expense and balance sheet reports, reports to funding agencies, and development and monitoring of organizational and contract or grant budgets.

- Oversee all purchasing and payroll activities for staff and participants.

- Develop and maintain systems of internal controls to safeguard financial assets of the organization and oversee federal awards and programs. Oversee the coordination and activities of independent auditors, ensuring all A-133 audit issues are resolved and all 403(b) compliance issues are met, and that the preparation of the annual financial statements is in accordance with U.S. GAAP and federal, state, and other required supplementary schedules and information.

- Attend Board and Subcommittee meetings, including being the lead staff on the Audit or Finance Committee.

- Monitor banking activities of the organization.

- Ensure adequate cash flow to meet the organization's needs.

- Serve as one of the trustees, and oversee administration and financial reporting of the organization's Savings and Retirement Plan.

- Investigate cost-effective benefit plans and other fringe benefits which the organization may offer employees and potential employees, with the goal of attracting and retaining qualified individuals.

- Oversee the production of monthly reports, including reconciliations with funders and pension plan requirements, as well as financial statements and cash flow projections for use by Executive management, as well as the Audit or Finance Committee and Board of Directors.

- Assist in the design, implementation, and timely calculations of wage incentives, commissions, and salaries for the staff.

- Oversee Accounts Payable and Accounts Receivable and ensure a disaster recovery plan is in place.

- Oversee business insurance plans and health care coverage analysis.

- Oversee the maintenance of the inventory of all fixed assets, including assets purchased with government funds (computers), assuring all are in accordance with federal regulations.

## *Required Knowledge, Skills, and Abilities*

The CFO must have knowledge of

- Not-for-profit accounting, in accordance with U.S. Generally Accepted Accounting Principles; OMB Circulars A-133, A-110, and A-122; TANF program regulations and compliance requirements; and appropriate Code of Federal Regulations sections.

- Current trends, developments, and theories in job readiness training and adult education.

- Current trends and developments in welfare reform, and the development of Welfare-to-Work programs under the DHHS TANF and other federal programs.

- Issues, concerns, and barriers of employees newly entering the workforce.

- Laws, regulations, and rules governing work requirements for TANF participants.

- Resources of public and private social service and related agencies.

- Organizational development, human resources, and program operations.

- General office software, particularly the Microsoft Office Suite and MIP software (or other similar not-for-profit general ledger software), and use of databases.

The CFO must have the ability to

- Foster and cultivate business opportunities and partnerships.

- Create and assess financial statements and budget documents.

- Recognize and be responsive to the needs of all clients of the organization, including funding organizations, the Board of Directors, local community advocates, participants, and employers.

- Supervise staff, including regular progress reviews and plans for improvement.

- Communicate effectively in both written and verbal form.

## *Education and Experience*

### EDUCATION

- Completion of a bachelor's degree at an accredited college or university, or equivalent work experience

- Completion of a master's degree at an accredited college or university, or equivalent work experience

- Certified Public Accountant (CPA) preferred

### EXPERIENCE

- The Controller or Chief Financial Officer level

- Five to seven years of financial experience and management experience with the day-to-day financial operations of an organization of at least 50 staff persons.

- Two years of direct service delivery experience working with long-term unemployed adults.

Any equivalent combination of education and experience determined to be acceptable.

## The Need for a Contract Controller or CFO

| **Answer This Question** |
| --- |
| What reasons could a firm have for wanting a contract finance leader? |

**Companies in transition are the usual customers for a contract Controller or CFO.**

While there is no written definition of what a contract financial executive is, it is accepted that this is a person who is hired to fill the role of Controller or CFO but is not a regular employee.

This person could be

- A CPA firm employee out on loan.

- An experienced Controller in between jobs.

- An independent contractor.

- An employee of a temporary or outsourcing agency.

- A person who has a business as a consulting Controller for several companies.

- A specialist in IPOs, mergers, systems, recapitalizations, or specific industry.

Whatever forms this relationship takes, there are four clear conditions:

1. The person is filling a pressing and urgent need.

2. The company has a reason for not making the position permanent.

3. The company needs the person to have a positive and quick impact.

4. The duration of the job is limited.

## *Most Common Reasons a Company Employs a Contract Financial Executive*

The most common reasons a company employs a contract financial executive include:

- They lack the funding.

- Rapidly changing business conditions.

- The company does not see the need.

- The incumbent is out on leave.

- The company is in transition or flux.

- The company needs a high-level employee for a short-term project.

- The company is undecided about the position in its long-term strategy.

## The Role of the Contract Controller

Whatever the reason, condition, or structure, one thing is very clear and needs to be understood by the person filling the role of contract Controller:

**The company has a problem and is looking for you to solve it!**

This puts tremendous pressure on the Controller because:

**You are very visible and expected to produce quick results!**

This was not something that I was expecting when I initially became a Controller.

## *Positional Power*

In my first tenure as a Controller, I served as the Controller of a small family business. Sometime, within the first 90 days, an employee asked for my opinion about an existing company policy. Being an opinionated sort of fellow, I shared my view. The next day, the word was out about "Ron's new policy." I was surprised by this outcome and I surely was not paying attention.

Several months later, again I was asked my opinion about something that was not an official policy. Of course, I expressed my thoughts. By the next day, "Ron's new policy" was instituted. This time I paid attention!

Controllers and CFOs carry a mantle of leadership authority. My opinion carried the weight of official policy, which I failed to realize the first time I expressed it. After the second incident, I became very careful about expressing my thoughts in informal settings regarding what the company should and should not do. Being a small business, most of our policies were more of a procedure or custom than an official written document.

There is nothing wrong with sharing an opinion as an employee. However, the mantle of authority we are given has a significant impact on other employees. Coming from public accounting where the partners made all the rules, it never occurred to me that I would be thrust into the rule-making responsibility as their first Controller.

Since 1988, whenever I share this story with other Controllers, I get at least one person who tells me they had a similar experience. So I take some comfort in knowing that I am not the only one who failed to realize the visibility and power the Controller has in an organization.

Whether you are a Controller in a part-time, full-time, or contract capacity you too will be carefully observed by every employee. With non-executive employees, each of your actions and decisions carry a lot more weight than you realize.

Realize it. Accept it. Capitalize on this critical visibility and authority!

---

**Activity 3-2: Perils of Pauline, Part 4**

Despite your advice against it, Pauline still wants to be a contract Controller. Using the tremendous laundry list of job responsibilities (see chapter 1, exhibit 1-1), explain your understanding of the true role of a contract financial executive.

---

## Valuing and Choosing the Appropriate Role for You

### *Varying Roles of the Hired Gun*

As a Hired Gun, you can either choose the role that brings out the best in you or let the client define a role for you. In table 3-1, you can see that there are multiple levels within each role that the contract CFO and contract Controller can play.

Take the time to study table 3-1 and see which one matches what you want to accomplish as a contractor or part-timer. Please pay attention to how much the rates vary in each role.

**Table 3-1: Comparison of the Varying Roles of the Contract CFO and Contract Controller**

| Contract CFO | | |
|---|---|---|
| **Role** | **Description** | **Hourly Rates*** |
| Owner Advisor | Works closely with the organization's owner(s) and becomes their personal counselor. Seeks external financing for growth, recapitalization, or planned IPO. | $100 - $150 |
| Strategist | Assists in establishing overall strategy that the firm must take to be successful. This role is required in small companies that have absentee leadership, or where the owners lack ability to think and act strategically. | $100 - $150 |

| Compliance Officer | Serves as the bad cop in the organization, where no one else serves that purpose. | $75 - $100 |
|---|---|---|
| **Contract Controller** | | |
| **Role** | **Description** | **Hourly Rates** |
| Chief Operating Officer Controller | Assists in non-traditional matters and serves as a key member of leadership team. Usually found in small organizations. | $100 - $200 |
| Financial or Acting CFO Controller | Operates as CFO, in addition to administrating typical accounting functions. | $75 - $100 |
| Operational Controller | Helps manage the organization, in addition to administrating accounting functions. This role is required in a small company with absentee leadership or an owner with limited leadership role. | $50 - $75 |
| Accounting Controller | Does bookkeeping and accounting grunt work. Often found in large organizations. | $25 - $50 |

\* The hourly rates are for comparison only. The rates do not constitute the amount that you could expect to be paid, because each engagement and situation is different. The rates do, however, indicate the typical value that a hiring organization places on the specific role they ask the Hired Gun to play.

## Conclusion

Not every organization has a need for a Controller or CFO to work under contractor status. Those that do need someone to be very effective during a time of extreme transition. As a contractor, not only will you wear the mantle of authority granted to a permanent employee, but you will be expected to fulfill all those responsibilities, as well.

Unless you want to work long days and nights, it is wise for you to avoid getting sucked into the Controller's Vacuum. The best way to avoid this phenomenon is to proactively take charge of the responsibilities that you choose to undertake, and find ways to delegate or distribute those that pull you into the vacuum.

In chapter 5, you will be shown the specific tool which will help you avoid a contractor's nightmare of working 50 hours per week, while only getting paid for 25.

Successful consulting projects are goal-oriented, narrowly defined, limited in duration, and contain standards of accountability.

For the client, hiring a contract professional can be a cost effective alternative to hiring a full-time staff.

# Chapter 4

# Attitudes for Success

**Your attitude determines your altitude! You determine your attitude.**

## Introduction

Without knowing who you are, I can guarantee that you already have the technical and other skills that you need to be successful. However, there are two attitudes that separate those who are successful in this contractor position from those who are not. These attitudes also apply to the person who chooses to serve as a part-time CFO or Controller.

The first attitude will improve as you take on more projects. Quickly developing this attitude, which I coin as "Teflon-coated mental toughness," will serve you in many ways.

A duck is considered waterproof, as are most birds. The duck can stay in frigid waters and not feel the cold or damp. This waterproofing describes the first attitude that will help your success as a Hired Gun. This is not to say that you lack this. You also do not lack the three sights that make up the Fortune Teller Attitude.

The Fortune Teller Attitude is the awareness that you have a tremendous amount of knowledge that you can use at any time. Use your hindsight, foresight, and insight in ways that benefit your client.

This chapter serves as a reminder that you will need both of these attitudes and for you to reinforce them occasionally.

> Accountants on Call is a New Jersey based firm that specializes in placing financial temporaries from accounting clerks to CFOs.
>
> "Accountants have high-level skill sets and we perform value-added services when we place them."

> Outsourcing firms such as Emerald Business Solutions of Scottsdale, Arizona serve companies in need of quality business information. "The irony of small business is that many small business owners need the most advice when they can afford it the least."
>
> Firms like Emerald provide clients with a permanent, part-time, or full-time CFO or Controller who spends time on the client's premises.

> Ohio based SS&G Financial Services finds firms that require outsourcing services or companies that have their financial information in shambles. SS&G Financial Services began in 2000 and hires only people from industry and not those from public accounting.
>
> Why do many outsourcing and contracting firms prefer the professional from industry over the professional from public? It is a complaint I hear every day.
>
> Reasoning: The public CPA only knows the theory of the problem, while the industry person knows where the skeletons are buried. Industry CPAs have been involved in solving the problems many times.

After completing this chapter you should be able to

- Define the plusses and minuses of being a contractor instead of an employee.

- Explain how you benefit by redefining yourself as your own employer and boss.

- Know how to adopt the attitude of Teflon-coated mental toughness.

- Understand why you must stay away from office politics and meetings.

- Recognize the reasons that it is easy to blur the role between contactor and employee.

- Use your three special sights to make you indispensable as a resource.

## What Mindset Does the Contract Controller Need?

> **Answer This Question**
>
> What do you see as the benefits and costs of being a gun for hire?

Please see exhibit 4-1 for an example of the advantages and disadvantages of the contract controller position.

> **Answer These Questions**
>
> List some of the soft costs that the person considering being a contract Controller needs to consider.
>
> List some of the soft costs that the person considering being a part-time Controller needs to consider.

## Contractor's Mindset

For those of you reading this book who work for a public accounting firm and are contracted out to a client as their unofficial Controller, this discussion of the contractor's mindset will seem unnecessary.

Please keep in mind that a majority of CPAs who choose to be a contract Controller were once regular everyday employees. For many of them this is likely their first opportunity to serve as a contractor or consultant who accepts the responsibilities that the everyday Controller has. They need a gentle reminder that they are a consultant.

As a Hired Gun, you will sit in the Controller or CFO's chair for 20 to 50 hours a week and perform all the normal functions that an employee does, you will interact with employees as an employee does, you will be vital to the organization's success. Yet you get compensated by the hour. You will naturally become emotionally tied to your client. If you were an employee prior to becoming a contractor, you developed emotional connections to your employers; you were loyal to them and respected them.

You find yourself in a position doing everything their employee would do except the terms of your employment relationship are different.

Not everyone needs this reminder. In my interactions with the scores of Hired Guns whom I have had the pleasure to meet since 1992, 75 percent of them needed this reminder about the contractor's mindset.

There are more reasons why someone like you who is contemplating being a Hired Gun must adopt a different attitude.

**Exhibit 4-1**

**The Pluses and Minuses of the Contract Controller Position**

| Advantages | |
| --- | --- |
| **For You:** | **For the Hiring Company:** |
| ☐ flexibility | ☐ flexibility |
| ☐ less commitment | ☐ less commitment |
| ☐ new challenges and skills | ☐ lower cost |
| ☐ immediate impact | ☐ immediate impact |
| ☐ constantly marketing yourself | ☐ higher caliber person |
| ☐ life balance | ☐ higher caliber talent and skills |
| ☐ excitement | ☐ "just in time" help |
| ☐ less pressure | ☐ low risk |
| ☐ no political games | ☐ no emotional attachment to job |

| Disadvantages | |
| --- | --- |
| **For You:** | **For the Hiring Company:** |
| ☐ undependable source of income | ☐ recruitment time |
| ☐ selecting the right company | ☐ selecting the right candidate |
| ☐ little notice of termination | ☐ higher cost |
| ☐ lack of stability | ☐ lack of stability |
| ☐ constant marketing of yourself | ☐ less reliance on one employee |
| ☐ focus on short-term solutions | ☐ focus on short-term solutions |
| ☐ little or no benefits | ☐ consultant may need time to fit in |
| ☐ high risk | ☐ limits on contractor's time and availability |

## *1. You Control Your Own Destiny*

### THE GREAT JOB RECESSION OF 2008-2010

In the past three years, over eight million jobs have been eliminated. Many of these may never return.

#### *Semi-permanent Unemployment*

In Washington State alone, over 200,000 accountants, finance managers, bankers, construction employees, and blue collar specialists lost their full-time jobs. It will take years for those jobs to come back, if they return at all. A majority of these laid off workers, who have degrees, experience, and useable skills, are unable to find meaningful work. In this Great Job Recession, the average time for being out of work has exploded from several months to years.

#### *Denial*

The problem when it comes to losing your job is that you can easily slip into a state of denial, believing that this is only a temporary condition.

#### *Self-Esteem Concerns*

When your job disappears, you lose a support system that is often your reason for living —a sort of external motivator. Far too many employees invest their lives in their careers and, unfortunately, define themselves by a job or career. If you often introduce yourself by saying "I am a CPA" or "I am an accountant," then you probably have fallen into this mindset, as well. Therefore, your self-esteem suffers when your job or career is taken from you.

#### *The Retirement Gap*

Only a few years ago, nearly 40 percent of employees at large and medium-size companies had a guaranteed pension plan. Today, only 15 percent of workers have any sort of guaranteed retirement benefits. This retirement gap extends from the Boomers, who are close to retirement, all the way to those in their twenties, who are just joining the work force.

### TRANSFORMATION OF JOBS AND PAY

Currently, we are in a major disruption and restructuring of the workforce, about work itself, and how workers and their pay are defined. Just like today, America and the rest of the world have gone through several of these major jobs transformations in the past.

One of the first job transformations was when we changed from a nation subsisting on agriculture and sole proprietors to one that relied on huge businesses and factories that mass-produced products. The next transformation was when these large factories were shuttered and the jobs were moved to second-world countries while, locally, service jobs replaced blue collar jobs. Again, a smaller disruption occurred when jobs were redefined and paychecks depended upon one's ability to employ technology and one's degree or education.

## 2. You Are Your Boss and Employer

No one knows for sure exactly what redefinement of work and pay we are moving towards, but it is clear that most of the jobs that exist today and have existed in the past ten years (for example, bank tellers, research assistants, librarians, journalists, draftsmen, and cashiers) are being phased out of existence.

The solution is to see yourself as an independent contractor instead of a regular and full-time employee. In order to do this, you must accept the premise that you most likely will not work for just one employer for more than a few years, and may work several jobs simultaneously.

You must also believe that you will work in a specific career or profession for only a decade or so, before finding another one with a future. Finally, you must recognize that you are in control of your employment destiny.

WAYS TO FINE TUNE YOUR ATTITUDE

A few things you can do to help you adopt this "I Am My Own Employer" attitude are

- Establish ownership for all your work and work products.

- Define your unique assets or talents, past and present.

- Prove your worth to your existing employer every day.

- Continually reinvent yourself by investing in learning new things.

- Seek out the ways that your current skills are transferable to other professions.

- Create a positive focal point in your life that is outside of work, such as a hobby or avocation.

## The Attitude of Teflon-Coated Toughness

To be a successful advisor and worker, the contract and part-time Controller needs to develop a mental toughness.

This toughness is required because you will find yourself stuck in the middle on many issues.

Your client's leaders will look to you for advice and counsel but will also treat you as an outsider or worse, a management spy.

It is hard for most people to feel comfortable in this insider/outsider role. Many contract and part-time Controllers are asked to work themselves out of a job, which is a painful experience.

I coined the term for this mindset using the metaphor of Teflon, which is a material that holds up to heavy use and high temperatures. Yet, Teflon keeps a smoothness that prevents sticking. By putting Teflon with the word toughness, it describes an attitude of being supportive, concerned, and caring, yet being able to stay emotionally unattached.

## Reasons for This Attitude

These are the many reasons you need Teflon-coated mental toughness. Some are expected, while a few are strange but true.

- You are a contractor serving as an employee, which puzzles some employees.

- Employees do not understand your role or why you were not hired as an employee.

- The person who hired you may not have explained why you were hired.

- The person you work for may have built up tremendous expectations about what you can do.

- Employees have a natural wariness when dealing with consultants.

- Members of the accounting team often think that you are there to take their jobs away.

- Besides results, the client is looking to you for specific advice on how to improve things.

- The client and their employees know that each time they talk with you it is costing the company money; so they try to have very little interaction with you.

- You may fill the seat of an employee who is popular and is missed.

- No one quite understands your authority or why you are asking them to do things for you.

- You are asked to supervise and direct employees, yet you are not their official supervisor.

- You may be required to give accounting employees a performance evaluation, yet you have only worked with them for a short period of time and will be gone soon.

- You are not always available when they need you, which can be unsettling to some employees.

- You stay focused and on task and do not participate in normal office activities, yet you are in the office every day.

- Finally, you are a high-powered CPA, yet you are not the auditor. *So why are you there?*

> **Answer This Question**
>
> As a gun for hire, how do you strive to develop this mental toughness?

## How to Develop a Tough, Non-Stick Attitude

Tips for developing a tough, non-stick attitude include

- See yourself as an outside advisor.

- Keep a mental distance from those within.

- Remind yourself and others of what your role is.

- Keep up your networking activities.

- Expect to be asked to leave at any time.

## SEE YOURSELF AS AN OUTSIDE ADVISOR

As I stated earlier, you need to understand that you are hired as an outsider. Most of the time, what your client expects from you is clarity. It could be clear thinking on what is not working or new ideas on how to improve what is currently being done.

Falling into the employee mode is easy for someone who is hired as a contractor for the first time.

One of the Hired Guns I coach was an employee for over 25 years and is in his second year as a contract professional. Six months into every new project, he forgets that he is an outside advisor. When I notice this, I remind him that his client wants specific suggestions about improvements that regular employees are missing. After many reminders, he develops a long list of specific things that his client can do to make things more productive. He recognizes his habit and appreciates my gentle reminder to see himself as an outside advisor.

## KEEP A MENTAL DISTANCE FROM THOSE WITHIN

Look back at the laundry list of reasons that you need to develop a Teflon-coated mental toughness. Most of them are related to how the people you work with will relate to and perceive you. You also must remind yourself on a regular basis to keep a mental distance from those you work with.

Here are a few suggestions that helped me and other contractors:

- Prepare a weekly report for your client on the achievements you have made for them.

- Develop a written "suggestions for improvement" report and present this to your client on a regular basis.

- Excuse yourself from most staff, office, or company meetings that have nothing to do with your role.

- Avoid the normal office chitchat that happens in hallways and after meetings.

- Do not go to lunch with employees on a regular basis unless it is for a business reason.

- Refrain from attending office parties.

- Do not get involved with the office grapevine.

- If you are on a long-term assignment (over three years), decline from receiving longevity or milestone recognition.

- If you are on a long-term assignment do not participate in employee of the month recognition.

## REMIND YOURSELF AND OTHERS OF WHAT YOUR ROLE IS

As I stated earlier, your client will probably do one of two things. He will probably not explain the specific reasons why you are hired or will play up your background and accomplishments as the reasons you are hired.

The first scenario will create a tremendous amount of skepticism and wariness about why you are there. Employees, when they are in a difficult situation, worry that they will be terminated. Suddenly, you show up as the expert and their fear escalates.

The second scenario also creates a tremendous amount of skepticism and wariness about you specifically. Employees have a natural fear of consultants and the more that your client builds you up, the more of a target you become.

This strategy will help you in these two scenarios and will serve to get you out of unnecessary expectations that others will place upon you.

> **Example:** You are a stand-in for their regular Controller who is out on family leave. This person, whose chair you sit in, spends hours each day answering employees' questions. In your capacity, as a consultant who is expected to streamline the accounting department, you cannot afford to spend half of those precious hours solving other people's problems.
>
> Employing this strategy whenever someone comes to you with a question, you can ask: "Does this issue have to do with streamlining the accounting department?" If the answer is "no," then you tactfully inform them: "My sole purpose for being here is to improve our accounting processes. All my energy and time is focused on that goal." You then suggest other people who can offer assistance.
>
> I find this to be a very common issue that all Hired Guns face. Employees will use the contract Controller or CFO as their sounding board and crutch. This habit is detrimental to your success as a Hired Gun.

## KEEP UP YOUR NETWORKING ACTIVITIES

A good strategy for keeping your mental distance and seeing yourself as an outsider is to spend a few minutes each day networking with others which serves you in two ways. First, you have the opportunity to use other professionals as your sounding board for the issues that you are currently facing and the opportunity to return the favor. Second, you will soon be out of a job and you need to be on the lookout for your next project or client.

Daily networking will keep you informed about potential work. Feedback from all Hired Guns shows that this business is very cyclical. For several months of the year you will be so busy that you do not have time to breathe. For several months of the year you have very little to do and are worried when the next project will fall into your lap.

By establishing a daily habit of networking by maintaining contacts and making new connections, you will be able to reduce the wild swings in your project work flow.

EXPECT TO BE ASKED TO LEAVE AT ANYTIME

This final strategy may seem superfluous to those who have been contracting for a while and those who work in public accounting. However, this was a painful mistake that I made in my first Hired Gun position. I want others to learn from my mistakes.

MY STORY

For over a decade, I was a Controller and then a CFO in the regular employee capacity. My first opportunity to work under contract popped up unexpectedly. This was not even in my radar but I took a chance. The project was open-ended since the client did not know how long the project would last. About six months into the project, my client Bob, the CEO, came into the office I occupied and said, "Ron, your last day will be in two weeks. It has been great having you here but the shareholders have decided that we can no longer afford to have a CFO."

My face fell and I tried to hide my disappointment. To me it felt like I was being fired, a painful experience for anyone. Bob noticed the look on my face and said, "Ron, you knew this day was coming. Why are you disappointed?" I assured him that everything was okay and that I understood completely.

As I sat back trying to understand why I was feeling rejected, it hit me. I was emotionally attached to the company. Even though I came in as a contractor, I maintained the attitude of an employee. I had not realized this because it was a habit formed by 25 years of employee status. So, when I developed this book, I purposely listed my mistake as a warning sign to others who are considering becoming a contractor.

## The Attitude of the Fortune Teller

The second attitude that you need to be successful is what I coined as the Fortune Teller Attitude. This is the willingness to openly and confidently use your hindsight, foresight, and insight.

Pretend that you have concerns about your future so you visit a fortune teller. She hands you a cup of tea—after you pay her fee—and you talk about your issues and concerns. After finishing your tea, she takes your cup and pours the tea leaves onto a plate. She proceeds to read your future by studying the tea leaves.

This *expert* you have engaged is using her gift of three special sights to help you sort out what you need to do.

*Hindsight*

| **Answer This Question** |
| --- |
| Cite an example where you recently used hindsight to solve a problem or avoid one. |

The fortune teller has years of experience and wisdom behind her. If she is any good she has heard about nearly every problem that a person could experience. The fortune teller uses the hindsight of her and others' experiences in advising you.

The normal person is said to have 20/20 hindsight. The Hired Gun must have 40/20: meaning you can quickly look at the past and identify trends and opportunities. You are experienced. You have been through all sorts of situations. You have listened to the stories of others in CPE sessions or in casual conversations. Believe it or not, your brain has stored all this data, which is accessible whenever you need it. The trick in the Fortune Teller Attitude is to trust yourself. You already know where you are headed. If you do not change your path (or deal with your problem), you know exactly where you will end up.

The first element of the Fortune Teller Attitude is to use your hindsight as an asset.

> **Example:** Before the recession that began in late 2007, many companies thought they had a sound Business Model, because they were profitable. But, once nearly every market shrunk like a balloon with a hole, they went out of business, because they had an irrelevant or outdated business structure or their strategies where flawed.
>
> The question to consider, using your hindsight, is this: *Will this pattern of denial continue, or will CEOs learn from this painful experience?*

## *Foresight*

---
**Answer This Question**

Cite an example where you recently used foresight to solve a problem or avoid one.

---

You assume that this fortuneteller has the gift of foresight. Yet, foresight is simply understanding the phenomenon of cause and effect. For every action there is a reaction. By paying attention, watching, observing, and testing you too can become an expert on cause and effect. The fortune teller knows this and relies on paying attention, watching, observing, and testing to amaze you with her foresight.

Foresight is not only the ability to think ahead and predict the future; it is also the courage to act on what you predict might take place. People in accounting prefer not to make mistakes, so we fail to act if we do not have sufficient information. The Fortune Teller Attitude requires courage because your trigger point for acting is much lower than your comfort level.

> **Example:** You are collecting data that will lead to an important decision, which needs to be made quickly. If no information is "0" and full information is "100," the time for you to act is at "60."
>
> The willingness to act sooner than later takes a tremendous faith in your own abilities and is a crucial element of this Fortune Teller Attitude.
>
> **Example:** The preliminary results of the 2010 election seem to indicate that small businesses will win, since the GOP claims to promote their interests. However, it is also clear Congress will hold any improvements to the economy hostage to get what they want —full control of all branches of the government. The question to consider, using your foresight, is this: *Will those who truly represent the interests of small businesses work cooperatively to make sure businesses have the means to prosper and hire people?*

*Insight*

> **Answer This Question**
> Cite an example where you recently used insight to solve a problem or avoid one.

The fortune teller tells you the meaning of the tea leaves because she deeply understands human nature. Believe it or not, people are predictable. We all have the same wants, desires, dreams, hopes, and fears. The fortune teller uses this knowledge or insight to say the things that will make you believe what she says is true. Even before your appointment with the fortune teller, you already knew what you needed to do; you just could not admit it to yourself.

The third element of the Fortune Teller Attitude is insight. All too often accountants tend to take things at face value or rely only on numbers. You give a financial statement to a client without saying anything. You hand a batch of reports to the executive committee without comment. You prepare a special analysis report for someone who requested it and never take the time to reveal the insights that you gleaned from your work.

As a person with a deep background of financial accomplishments, you have tremendous insight that very few other people in your organization or business have. It is our gift and yet for some reason we are timid in sharing this insight. The people in business who get the highest financial rewards are those who are willing to share their insights and the courage to stand behind them.

> **Example:** I recently consulted with a professional services firm that had high employee turnover and was not profitable all year round —only in busy season. Using your insight, the question to consider is this: *Are issues such as turnover, dissension, and lack of employee engagement problems or symptoms?*
>
> Using my insight, I knew that those were symptoms and not the cause of the problem. After asking lots of questions and looking at the firm objectively, I found that the problems were caused by the culture. Once we made sure all the partners supported one culture and a unified set of values, these lingering problems vanished.

PUTTING THEM ALL TOGETHER

The fortune teller, who some people assume has the ability to read the future, is merely a person using the three elements that you need to be successful as a contract Controller or CFO:

- Hindsight

- Foresight

- Insight

## Conclusion

Because you are filling the position of Controller, one that may have been or could be occupied by a regular employee, you must first recognize that you are an independent agent brought in to solve a problem. Yet with all the responsibilities that the typical Controller has, it is easy for the Hired Gun to fall into an employee mindset.

This mindset, which can be described as, "I love solving problems and I am always here to help!" can make you ineffective and especially unproductive. To be successful as a contract professional, you must develop an attitude of Teflon-coated mental toughness.

Before you can fully recognize the importance of this attitude, it is good to review the advantages and disadvantages of going into a contractor situation. You are the only one who can determine if the advantages outweigh the negatives or the reverse.

The Fortune Teller Attitude reminds you to use three special sights to help both your client and you solve the client's issues. You already have the gifts of hindsight, foresight, and insight. See these as something beneficial and valuable.

Now that you have a good understanding of these two key attitudes, we will quickly move into the skills that ensure your success as a Hired Gun.

# Chapter 5

# How Can I Ensure I Will Be Successful?

**The crisis of today is the joke of tomorrow!**

## Introduction

After completing this chapter you should be able to

- Administer the Howard Hughes test to your client.

- Develop and implement a Position Description for yourself.

- Structure your work and responsibilities so that you are doing what is most important.

- Focus on the client's metrics for performance.

- Identify and report on the client's Critical Success Factor.

- Keep out of the day-to-day minutiae that will detract from your effectiveness.

## No Guarantee of Success, So Improve Your Odds

Before we get into the specific skills, we need to spend some time on five best practices. Each practice is easy to adopt and very powerful. Combined, these practices will help you deliver what the client expects, while making you productive and effective.

Going into an opportunity where you are the contract Controller or CFO means that you will have some hard work to do. You will use the efforts of others to get there. Together these best practices build a structure that ensures your success.

Not every engagement that you undertake will require you to work at the strategic level. This fact does not excuse you from being able to think and act strategically, while understanding how a CEO views their business. We will start this chapter by seeing if you can pass the Howard Hughes Test in activity 5-1. If you fail this test you may want to reconsider whether you truly have the ability to be a contract Controller or contract CFO.

## Tactics for Creating Success as the Part-Time or Contract Hired Gun

There are five sure-fire best practices that will guarantee your effectiveness in the role of part-time or contract Controller. Each is a tactic that you need in your Hired Gun toolkit:

1. Define your role with a Position Description.

2. Determine what is most important.

3. Enhance their metrics of performance.

4. Help them fly in formation with their Critical Success Factor.

5. Keep your eyes on the forest.

---

**Activity 5-1: Take the Howard Hughes Test!**

Imagine that you are the Howard Hughes (owner) of your employer (or major client) and can access just one piece of information on a regular (hourly, daily, weekly, monthly) basis. This one data point will only tell you whether your firm or client is succeeding or not; it will not tell you to what degree. Get ready to write down what you need to know, but before you do...the information you receive cannot be

- Sales or revenues.

- Margins, of any kind.

- Profits.

- Cash flows.

- Share price.

- Any financial measurement.

**Answer quickly:**

*What information must you have to know if your firm is being successful?*

*What does this information tell you? Why did you select it?*

*Do you measure and include this in your regular daily, weekly, or monthly reporting?*

**The Bad News**

If you could not answer this without thinking of some financial metric: sales, profits, or cash flows, then you not only failed the HH test, you are not qualified to be an advisor to CEOs! Sorry!

You failed because you are not thinking like a CEO. What CEOs do best is know their business model so well that they can look at performance metrics like orders received or orders shipped and instantaneously translate that into how well the firm is doing. We financial-minded hold onto the metrics—like a mussel holds onto the pier—that are of little value to operational-minded managers. They just care about how much inventory we have and how old the receivables are because *we tell them* they should care.

To be a good consultant, you need to let go of your dependence on the Balance Sheet and Income Statement and delve more into the real performance that your client's managers care and worry about.

---

## *Lessons from the HH Test*

Knowing and helping your client understand the client's Critical Success Factors will make you invaluable.

The purpose of the Howard Hughes Test is to remind you, as the financial contract professional, that you must find and report on what is important. Of course your challenge is refining and honing in on what is important for your client or employer. Different people in the organization will have different definitions of what they feel is "most important." The best way to deal with this challenge is to administer to each manager the Howard Hughes Test. Based upon what they tell you they need to know, then that becomes what you measure and report on for them.

As the Controller or CFO, you must get out of the habit of reporting financial metrics and the historical information you currently report. You must begin to transform your monthly reports into a feedback tool that provides key metrics to decision-makers on a daily, weekly, and of course monthly basis. Some Controllers are finding that in order for their employer to keep up with the competition or marketplace, they are required to report on some key data hourly.

The best way to make this transformation easy and effective is to add performance metrics into the reports that you prepare. Performance metrics, which will be defined next, must be those things that measure what is important within your organization. Not all the metrics need to come through accounting. Some will come from the operational employee's own databases. You will match those statistics with your financial data in order to give the decision-makers valuable insight: actual performance and how it translates into sales, costs, or profits.

Get over the fear that you will not be able to audit their numbers and that one of their bad numbers in your reports will harm your credibility. As their vendor of information, you must spend time with each person who keeps their own database of operational data and understand where their numbers come from and how they are generated. After understanding that the numbers are wholesome, you must give them the smell test each time you include them in your reports. This requires you to *really* know and understand what is going on in every aspect of your client's product or service cycle. This is also the responsibility of a financial professional. Get out of your office each day, walk around, and talk to people who are unfamiliar with accountanese.

## Tactic 1: Define Your Role

**Consultant's motto: Time is revenue!**

Unless you proactively negotiate for the support you need to accomplish what the client asks, you will not be successful! An extremely powerful tool that you can use to define the role and support is a Position Description.

## *Hired Gun Tool: A Position Description*

A Position Description is much more than a typical job description. It is a tool and best practice that helps you to fully define a job and put emphasis on what the company wants—*results*. These are clearly defined in the Expected Results section.

## ELEMENTS OF THE POSITION DESCRIPTION

Elements of the Position Description include

- Qualifications for the job

- Specific job duties

- Expected results from the employee

- Impact of the job on the organization

- Authority levels for the position

- Specific difficulties the person may have

- Interpersonal relationships

- Any other key items necessary for success

While having a job description is something every Hired Gun and member of the support team should have, the Position Description will enable the leading-edge Controller to be very successful. This assurance comes from proactively defining your role for the client using the above elements. The emphasis on a typical job description is on the duties, while the focal point of the Position Description is on the *expected results*. By emphasizing these, you eliminate the need to cram every conceivable task in the specific duties.

This approach really pays off when you use this tool on the marginally successful employee who hides under their reasoning: "But that task is not in my job description!" By defining what you expect of them, you eliminate this popular excuse and self-limiting belief.

### *Expected Results*

You define and get your client's (employer's) agreement on what these are before you get deep into the job.

This section helps you stay focused.

### *Impact on the Organization*

You agree with your client (employer) on obtaining the resources you need so that you can have the impact desired and achieve the expected results.

This clarification helps in your leadership role.

### *Authority Levels*

You define what decisions you can and cannot make and ask for those that will support you in getting the expected results.

This definition helps you to know what is really important.

*Special Difficulties*

You spell out those things which will limit your ability to get quick or lasting results, like needing to upgrade the technical skills of your existing staff or having to invest in new technology. The things identified here are usually those limitations that *could* prevent you from getting the expected results.

This section helps you and your client (employer) to be mutually accountable to each other.

*Interpersonal Relationships*

You agree with your client (employer) on the people that you have responsibility to and for, whom you regularly communicate with, and where you fit into the organization's structure.

This helps you to keep your eyes on the big picture and see the forest.

## BENEFITS OF USING A POSITION DESCRIPTION

Why should you have a PD for yourself and each member of your support team?

The client, or employer, may expect you to accomplish things without giving you the support and authority to get it accomplished. The Position Description will enable you to quickly determine what you need so that you can negotiate for them. This is your biggest benefit for using a Position Description in your engagement, but that is not the only one.

The other payoffs are numerous, and here are some specific ones. A Position Description

- Communicates clear expectations to everyone.
- Clarifies goals in advance.
- Reduces overlaps and gaps among the many employees' duties and responsibilities.
- Reduces uncertainty about what is expected.
- Documents performance because it is the basis for evaluations.
- Shortens the learning curve for new employees.
- Gives a clear definition of the job requirements to any applicant.
- Helps you keep your eyes on the forest.

## TIPS ON MAKING THE POSITION DESCRIPTION EFFECTIVE

The following tips will help make the Position Description effective.

*Results-Oriented*

Make the emphasis of everyone's PD on the results you expect from them. To ensure that the PD remains fresh and current, update every employee's PD at least semiannually or every time you conduct a performance evaluation, whichever comes sooner.

*Proactive*

Be sure that you state the expected results in a proactive manner. This encourages you and your employees to take the initiative and become more of a self-starter. This evolves your role of being more of an encouraging coach and less of a supervisor.

*Flexible*

By focusing everyone's attention on the expected results instead of their duties, you automatically instill greater flexibility in yourself and the employee. If you want to develop employees who remain proactive and seek out areas of adding value, then make each employee's PD flexible.

*Broad*

Today, the ideal employees are those that see the big picture, so it is important that you make the PD broad enough to cover more than just what the employee is doing currently. By developing their PD with a wide variety of expectations, you instill in the employee the need to see both the forest and the trees in their job.

Your own Hired Gun Position Description does not need to be broad. Only cover the current scope of your assignment.

*Brief*

The ideal PD is only one and a half pages long. As much as possible, you want to create a PD that is no more than two pages. If you can get the PD on one page, you make it even more effective and memorable; its length will depend on how many duties you include. Remember, the more you detail the expected results, the less you need to spell out in the specific duties.

---

**Exhibit 5-1**

**Position Description Template**

Name of Incumbent_____

Salary Grade_____

Position_____

Department or Team_____

**Qualifications:** Education, experience, specialized knowledge of skills. Personal qualities are not considered legitimate qualifications.

"4-year accounting degree with 2 to 4 years experience at supervisor level. Certified Public Accountant. One year experience in percentage-of-completion cost accounting."

**Expected Results:** Measurable standards of performance such as cost reduction or project deadlines.

"Implement computerization of General Ledger before July 1st."

---

> **Impact:** Amount of company assets the employee is accountable for including people, money, equipment, expense limits, or sales.
>
> "Lead a team of 10 professionals and manage a departmental budget of $500,000."
>
> **Authority:** Limitations (if any) on decisions made, approvals given, contract signing, hiring, and firing.
>
> "Accounts payable invoice approval up to $5,000. Travel expense voucher approval up to $1,000."
>
> **Principal Duties:** Major functional responsibilities.
>
> "Establish and monitor budgets for all departments."
>
> **Special Difficulties:** Problems or obstacles the employee has to overcome in achieving goals and producing the expected results.
>
> "Most action items are subject to strict deadline pressure."
>
> **Interpersonal Relationships:** Insiders and outsiders with whom the employee deals routinely, such as auditors, government agencies, colleagues, customers, or vendors.
>
> "Principal point of contact with our external auditors, the Department of Defense auditors, and agents from the IRS."

The following are examples of two Position Descriptions. One is for an Accounting Assistant and the other is for a part-time Controller.

## Example 5-1: Position Description Example for a General Accounting Assistant

*Qualifications*

The person filling this position will have a minimum of two years entry-level accounting experience or college education. They will have the interpersonal skills and problem-solving experience expected of a professional. Their technical knowledge will include, at a minimum, usage of PC based computer systems and related applications, knowledge and usage of Lotus 123® or Microsoft Excel®, e-mail, web searches, and database entry.

*Expected Results*

Within nine months of being on the job, the employee will have accomplished these goals:

- Show measurable improvements in accounts receivable collections, reducing Day Sales Outstanding (DSO) from the current 60 days to 35 days.

- After completing cross-training, have a good understanding of the duties and functions of accounts payable and payroll processing.

- Take over maintenance of general ledger and the preparation of related internal report package from the Controller.

## *Principal Duties*

- Timely collection of accounts receivable, including follow-up and documentation

- Accurate monthly inventory reconciliations

- Accurate monthly reconciliation of bank accounts

- In-depth analysis of general ledger accounts and preparation of detailed work papers

- Cross-training and understanding of duties in the following areas:

  - Accounts payable processing and transactions (that is, coding, processing payments, and so on)

  - Cash receipts processing and transactions (that is, coding, posting, reconciliation, and so on)

  - Sales processing and transactions (that is, invoicing, summarizing, posting, and so on)

  - Payroll processing and transactions (that is, data entry, tax filing, deposits, and so on)

- Other accounting-related duties and special projects as assigned and delegated.

## *Special Difficulties of the Position Description*

- Learning a complex accounting system quickly

- Working with a difficult accounting software and cost system

## *Interpersonal Relationships*

- Direct supervisor will be the Controller.

- Task supervisors will be Staff Accountant and the AP Specialist whenever cross-training and working within that person's area of responsibility.

- Person will also have daily contact with customers, bank employees, and company employees.

- Participating member of the finance team.

## *Evaluation and Feedback*

Quarterly performance evaluations will be made on the goals defined in the Expected Results and on the employee's learning curve in the following areas:

- Technical skills

- People skills

- Problem solving skills

- Professionalism

- Communication skills

- Speed in getting cross-trained

- Comprehension of training

- Attitude

- Enthusiasm

- Proactiveness

- Flexibility

- Willingness to learn

## Example 5-2: Position Description Example for a Part-Time Controller

### *Qualifications*

The person filling this role will have five years experience at the Controller level in a production specialty-company environment. The person will have supervised at least five employees, from the recruiting phase through termination. The incumbent will have achieved certification as a CPA or CMA.

### *Expected Results*

Within the next twelve months, the person is expected to

- Increase cash flows by 10 percent.

- Decrease DSO of accounts receivable by seven days.

- Speed up the delivery of financial and management reports by four days.

- Reduce accounting staff turnover and stay within the company-wide target of 10 percent.

### *Impact of Job on the Organization*

As a result of this person's role, Raelco will have competent financial leadership. The company's system of internal controls will be monitored and reported on annually. The person is expected to provide a positive management model for peers and a leadership model for finance employees.

## *Authority of Person to Act for the Company*

The Controller is authorized to sign checks without second signatory up to $5,000 and with second signatory up to $50,000. The person can make and approve purchases of non-inventory items up to $30,000. When drawing against the line of credit, the person can borrow up to $100,000 without the CEO's approval. The Controller can obligate Raelco to administrative type contracts of no longer than two years or a combined value of $6,000.

## *Special Difficulties of the Position*

Since this position is part-time (30 hours maximum per week), the Controller is expected to fully train staff and then delegate responsibilities and authority necessary to achieve goals and have the impact expected.

The Controller will need to fully understand the information systems, software, and hardware, since this person is responsible for the system's readiness.

The Controller will be required to have a good understanding of the job and the organization within six weeks.

## *Interpersonal Relations*

The Controller supervises all the finance employees, which include

- Accounts payable specialist.

- General ledger accountant.

- Accounts receivable specialist.

- Accounting clerks.

- Inventory specialist.

- Financial reporting specialist.

The Controller is a member of Raelco's senior management team, which consists of

- CEO,

- VP of Sales and Marketing,

- VP of Services,

- Director of Human Resources, and

- Director of Production.

The Controller will be the main or backup contact with these interested parties:

- Vendors

- Customers

- Banker or Loan Officer

- Legal Firm Partner

- CPA Firm Partner

- Leasing Company Representative

---

**Activity 5-2: Perils of Pauline, Part 5**

**Your Assignment:**

Read the "About Your Friend Pauline" section below. Pauline is in hot water and needs your help. You have agreed to be her coach. Keep in mind, Pauline will be expected to produce instant results. At then end, you should be able to answer the following two questions.

**Questions to Answer:**

1. What "Authority to Act" does Pauline need to have in order to be successful at resolving their issues? (Use the blank space left under "Authority of Person to Act for the Company" to fill in your answer.)

2. What are the "Special Difficulties" of the job that you would suggest Pauline define? (Use the blank space left under "Special Difficulties of the Position" to fill in your answer.)

**About Your Friend Pauline**

Pauline was just hired as the Controller under contract for the next 18 months by a fast-growing retail chain that has 21 locations scattered across the United States. Besides her meeting the qualifications, Pauline was hired because she was the audit manager with the Big 4 CPA firm that serves them. Rapid Jeweler's fast growth of 32 percent per year over the last 6 years has created significant problems, especially in timely financial reporting, inventory controls, and employees supporting one another.

Here are just a few of the issues that Mrs. Rapid, the CEO, expects Pauline to solve as quickly as possible:

- Inventory shrinkage currently runs between 3 percent to 4 percent (the yearly running average).

- Over the last 4 years, the accounting staff and the inventory control group experienced a turnover rate of over 25 percent.

---

- The inventory control group, who reports to the Controller, has well-trained employees. However since inventory management was not the forte of the prior Controller, he gave them very little direction and guidance. As a result they are both understaffed and undermanaged and this is one reason accounting has not adequately addressed the inventory shrinkage.

- A second major reason for the growth in inventory shrinkage is that the store manager's incentive plan rewards them for growing store sales and keeping store expenses low. They are not penalized for any inventory losses. They ignore the advice and controls suggested by the inventory control team.

The accounting group that Pauline will take charge of has worked valiantly to keep up with the dizzying growth spurts and their morale is poor. The accounting staff has grown from a single accountant seven years ago to a current staff of 16:

1—Accounting Manager and Acting-Assistant Controller
2—A/P Specialists
1—Cash Applications Specialist
2—Payroll Specialists
1—General Assistant
3—Store Operations Accountants
1—Inventory Control Manager
5—Inventory Control Specialists

The following is an excerpt from Pauline's recently developed Position Description:

**Rapid's Controller Position Description**

**Qualifications:**

The candidate will have 7 years experience at the Controller level in a retail company with multiple regional locations. The Controller will be skilled in inventory management, financial reporting, and multi-state taxation. The person will have supervised at least ten employees and facilitated a team process. The person filling the position will possess the following credentials: CPA, CMA, or MBA.

Interpersonal Relations:

- Supervises the Accounting Manager and the Inventory Control Manager.

- Indirectly guides the activities and performance for the general accounting staff (10 FTEs), and the inventory control staff (6 FTEs).

- Coordinates activity with the Executive Team—CEO, COO, Treasurer, VP of Stores, VP of Purchasing & Product Management, VP of Human Resources, and VP of Marketing Communications.

- Serves on the Management Committee consisting of peers, CEO, and COO.

**Expected Results:**

- Reduce inventory shrinkage to less than 1 percent of sales based on the current best practices in the jewelry industry.

- Increase the effectiveness of existing financial, store, and product controls.

- Get the Inventory Management group to take the lead on the inventory problems.

**Impact of the Job on the Organization:**

As a result of this position's leadership and visibility, the employees will have a proactive leader on ethical behaviors in handling inventory. Rapid's system of internal controls and shrinkage will be monitored and reported on a quarterly basis. The person is expected to provide a positive role model for peers and a leadership model for the finance team.

*What authority does Pauline need to accomplish what Mrs. Rapid wants?* Make any assumptions necessary to complete this description; just be sure to explain the reasoning behind those assumptions.

**Authority of Person to Act for the Company:**

*What challenges does Pauline face that she needs Mrs. Rapid to acknowledge?* Make any assumptions necessary to complete this description, just be sure to explain the reasoning behind those assumptions.

## LESSONS FROM THIS ACTIVITY

Mrs. Rapid wants Pauline to decrease the inventory shrinkage problem. Put yourself in her shoes when Mrs. Rapid informs Pauline:

"I hired you to fix accounting. You cannot change any of our compensation policies, only HR can do that. You may not visit the stores and talk with employees, because that is the VP of Stores' responsibility. I won't allow you to change any of our existing procedures. You may not fire any Rapid employees—we don't allow that sort of thing here.

One more thing: There is no money in your budget for travel or training."

**Anything Pauline attempts to do to "fix" the problem will fail! She is better off resigning or quitting.**

This can and will happen to you, unless you are given the correct amount of support and the appropriate authority to meet the expectations placed upon you.

From Pauline's situation, you can now see why you need the Position Description in your Hired Gun toolkit.

## Tactic 2: Determine What Is Most Important

**"Decide what you want, decide what you are willing to exchange for it. Establish your priorities and go to work."**

**H. L. Hunt**

| Answer This Question |
| --- |
| How do you determine what is most important within your organization? |

### *Find the Client's Pain!*

**The biggest challenge for the part-time or contract Controller is to determine where the urgency is needed in their firm or client.**

While their accounting system may be in shambles, there are probably other areas that are in worse shape. If solutions are not found quickly, the company could be in serious trouble (if it is not already).

EXAMINING THEIR PAIN REQUIRES TRUST IN YOU

When I mention their pain, it refers to the fact that your client's executives, managers, and employees have problems that are not getting resolved. As their Controller, you are the logical choice and most qualified person on whom they rely to help them get rid of their pain. You understand how the business operates, you understand how the finances work, and you (hopefully) understand the key players (that is, decision-makers) and what makes them tick. One of the most rewarding aspects of the job of the Hired Gun is to be regarded as the resource that employees think of first when they need a solution which they are unable to find themselves.

This does not mean that your coworkers and colleagues will get answers from you. What you will do best is employ your tools to help them find their own solutions. The last thing you want is to place yourself in a position where you cannot get your own work done because you are always solving everyone else's problems.

An effective way to get out of this productivity-eating situation is to see yourself as a consultant to others in the organization. A good consultant best serves their client when they enable the client to arrive at their own solution to a problem, one that instills accountability in them. In order to do this effectively, you must ensure that others trust you.

MEASURE THE IMPORTANT THINGS

Even though the basis for accounting is to account for things, not everything we count matters. This is one of the hardest lessons to learn for the CPA who moves from public accounting into the Controller or CFO's chair. In public accounting, we were brainwashed on dueling concepts of auditing the details, balancing to the penny, and ignoring the immaterial. This chapter includes five best practices that will enable you to serve your organization as the "CEO of an information business." That is how the accounting team must see itself—as a service business whose sole product is to provide quality and timely information through operational performance feedback.

## WAYS TO DETERMINE WHAT IS MOST IMPORTANT

Take the following actions so you will know where your help and expertise is needed:

- Meet with all the executives and managers, asking for frank assessments.

- Ask lots of open-ended questions as you inquire about how things are done.

- Ask "what-if" questions when learning about why things are done.

- Ask employees to describe their challenges.

- Talk with the company banker and CPA advisor.

- Perform analysis of recent financial and management reports.

- Develop a working model of how the company operates.

- Develop and use nonfinancial performance measures.

- Help the company understand and focus on its Critical Success Factor.

### *Meet with All the Executives and Managers for Frank Assessments*

Be sure to build into your project budget time to spend with as many executives and managers as possible during your first two weeks. Their insight combined with your financial acumen will give you information about what the client wants and needs.

Your biggest challenge will be to recognize if they are being honest with you.

### *Ask Lots of Open-Ended Questions About How Things Are Done*

For your first month on the project, do most of your communication in the form of open-ended questions. This will help you determine what is most important.

### *Ask "What-If" Questions When Learning About Why Things Are Done*

In addition to your open-ended questions, as you begin to understand how the client does things, remember to ask a lot of "what-if" questions. Employees who have been on their job for more than a year have a tendency to forget the reasons behind the work that they perform. Over time, employees have a tendency to repeat the same actions and decisions, without ever questioning why they are being done. For you to be successful in a contract role, you must understand the *why*.

As you go through each process, think about key "what-if" questions that will help you to identify changes that need to be made. If, within the first few weeks of your project, you can come up with several concrete recommendations that will improve profitability or increase productivity, your client will love you and discover how invaluable you are.

*Ask Employees to Describe Their Challenges*

Besides asking managers and other leaders about the problems and opportunities, remember to ask employees about these as well. In a dysfunctional organization (firms that are most likely to be your client), managers do not listen to employee suggestions and ideas. Over time, employees stop making suggestions.

By really listening to the employees you will get a long list of suggestions for change. Better yet you will turn employees into allies and resources.

*Talk with the Company Banker and CPA Advisor*

If the conditions call out for it, be sure to spend some time talking with the client's banker and their CPA firm. This is a tricky proposition and requires lots of tact and salesmanship. If the client is in trouble, hence the reason you are brought in, they may not want the banker to know how deep the problems go. It is important that their banker understands your role and why the client engaged you. This definitely will be a consideration if part of your responsibility is to prepare financial statements that go to the bank. We will cover the issue of independence in chapter 8.

Tact is also necessary when talking with the CPA advisor. If you were not sourced by their CPA firm, a bit of jealousy may be evident. I have experienced situations where the CPA firm was not cooperative with me because their ego was hurt. They were not asked to bid on the project. The CPA firm may misunderstand your role and think that you are trying to replace them.

Be sure to carefully explain why the client engaged you and their expectations of you. Many experienced contract Controllers and CFOs, after this air clearing conversation with the client's CPA, say they received full support and encouragement. "We are glad that they finally had the courage to get some professional help," is the sort of comment you may get from the CPA firm when their client is in deep trouble.

*Perform Analysis of Recent Financial and Management Reports*

Again, during your first few days of the project, spend time going through both their external and internal financial reports. Most Hired Guns tell me that they have a financial analysis protocol that they use for every client. Just going through the numbers and doing proper financial and ratio analysis will give you a clear understanding of both the client's problems and where you need to focus your efforts.

*Develop a Working Model of the Company's Operations*

A friend of mine, Gene, who has been doing contract CFO work since the mid-80s, only works with manufacturing companies. Prior to agreeing to work with a prospective client, he spends a day with them trying to put their business model into a financial spreadsheet. Gene told me, "If their CEO cannot describe his business in a way where I can build a financial model, then I do not want to work with that company. Their problems run deep, starting with the fact that the CEO does not understand the business."

About 15 percent of the Hired Guns I met over the years have a specific spreadsheet tool that they use to deeply analyze the client or prospective client. You might consider investing in such a resource, if you are serious and want to make a long-term commitment being a Hired Gun.

### Develop and Use Nonfinancial Performance Measures

Tactic 3 covers the best practice of performance measuring. As you go through and analyze your client's financial and operational states, remember to focus on the nonfinancial metrics. If a company is trying to pull the wool over the eyes of their banker, they will do it through the financial reports. It is in the operational statistics that you will find the truth that the client may be trying to hide.

### Help the Company Use its Critical Success Factor

In Tactic 4, the how and why of the Critical Success Factor best practice is explained.

## Why It's Hard to Find the "Real" Cause of an Issue or Problem

The real issues, which are the root cause of someone's lingering problems, are often hidden. They may be hidden behind a veil of smoke because of

- Excessive ego.

- Fear of failure.

- Fear of incompetence.

- True incompetence.

- Game playing for power.

Understanding why barriers exist and never go away by themselves aids the Hired Gun in seeing through them. In addition, there are two common pitfalls that contract or part-time professionals fall into. Once you are aware of them, you can avoid them.

#1 BIG MISTAKE OF THE HIRED GUN

**Not Defining the Problem Accurately.**

Information for defining the problem comes from

- Your personal knowledge.

- Your expertise.

- Discussions with the person that needs or demands the solution (that is, primary client).

- Discussions with the people who are impacted by the problem and who will be affected by the solution (that is, secondary clients).

- Gap Analysis or similar research.

- Investigation or audit of the systems, processes, and documents involved.

- Your intuition.

You may need to use all of these in defining the problem. The big mistake you make arises because you rely heavily on only one of them. You get comfortable in using what has worked for you in the past and hesitate to rely on other assets or tools. Look at this list and determine which of these talents or assets you rely most heavily on to the exclusion of the others.

#2 BIG MISTAKE OF THE HIRED GUN

**Not Using Others to Sound Out Your Reasoning or Logic.**

This big mistake occurs when you don't test your reasoning with others who are not involved in the problem. You fall into this trap for three reasons:

1. You are in a hurry.

2. You have not built or do not use a network of peers.

3. You do not think that you need to.

No matter how smart or experienced we are, we all need a way to sound out our reasoning or logic. Doing so is not an admission that you are incompetent, a feeling that most professionals have lounging in the back of their head. Rather, it is an enlightened view.

When you turn to someone who you trust and you know can remain objective, you are simply asking them to look for flaws or biases in your thought process. As human beings we all have biases. These assumptions about how life works interfere with your ability to be objective and inability to find the optimal solution to a problem.

Never be afraid to ask others to be your sounding board and to help you clarify your thinking so that you remain objective. This is an important trait of the contract professional.

> **Answer These Questions**
> Why would intuition be important to the Hired Gun?
> Why would having and using a sounding board be important to the Hired Gun?

## Tactic 3: Enhance Their Metrics of Performance

**"One accurate measurement is worth a thousand expert opinions."**

**Grace Hopper, Admiral US Navy**

Far too many businesses measure what is easy or what they think is important—growth, profits, or share price. By weaning the client off this dependency and helping them to find the proper solutions, you will be very successful.

## *Hired Gun Tool: Scorecard Metrics*

A major tool for the Controller who wishes to be of value to their client is the performance measurement process. This best practice of selecting, measuring, tracking, and reporting on them will show others that you think strategically and holistically.

### PERFORMANCE METRICS DEFINED

Let us examine performance measures by defining them, then determining what makes good ones.

A performance measure is a metric of an important activity, which is quantifiable, measurable, and meaningful. You use it as a yardstick that objectively measures achievement toward a specific business objective. The metric usually compares an input to an output.

Performance metrics can range from financial ones such as DSO, and 90 day AR, to operational ones such as inventory turn rate and scrap percentage, to customer-focused such as average number of daily customers and website hits, to process-related such as number of backorders and on-time delivery. There are even metrics to measure vendor performance and employee satisfaction.

The purposes of using performance metrics are to help decision-makers know quickly and accurately what is going on in their specialty and to help accounting do more situational analysis via trending and less variance reporting.

> **Example:** In the Electronic Distribution business, the key metric that everyone monitors is known as the "Book to Bill" ratio. This metric is Orders Received/Orders Shipped. The standard is "1." Having a "1" ratio means that the company is healthy, and any deviance from "1" means there is a potential problem that needs addressing immediately.

### CRITERIA OF A GOOD PERFORMANCE MEASURE

A good performance metric is more than just something that you can easily track or one your accounting system automatically generates. Metrics that measure what is important need to meet the following criteria:

- Focuses attention on a critical activity

- Is measurable

- Is monitored regularly

- Provides frequent and timely feedback or insight

- Includes a mix of financial and operational measurements

- Is simple to understand yet has the pulse on what is occurring on an hourly or daily basis

### GOALS OF USING PERFORMANCE MEASURES

Sadly, people have a short attention span. In addition, brain researchers tell us that we can only hold three or maybe four data points in our brain before we run out of bandwidth. In a nutshell, the goal of using performance measures for providing timely and quality feedback to others is to give report users simple data points that are meaningful and that they can remember. When they remember them and the metrics are meaningful, this greatly increases the likelihood that managers will pay attention to that metric.

Overall, these are the specific goals to justify that the Controller uses metrics in their reports. Performance measures

- Support the strategy by highlighting goals.

- Express measures for critical drivers.

- Express performance targets.

- Reduce confusion day-to-day.

COMPONENTS OF A GOOD PERFORMANCE MEASURE

Performance metrics are both simple and complex. The simplicity is that the metric measures one activity or event. The complexity occurs when you put two or more simple metrics together and they create an index or benchmark. The components of a performance metric include

- The Input(s).

- The Output(s).

- A Method of Measuring.

- A Degree of Measurement—Quality or Quantity based.

- An Assessment of the Measure—as expected or unexpected.

MEASUREMENT COMPONENTS

In order to use metrics wisely and effectively, the Controller and the finance team must ensure these six components exist:

1. The Inputs must be clean, meaning that any errors or faulty assumptions are corrected before the data goes into the transformation process (that is, if the month-end A/R balance is understated then the metric of 3 percent 90 days is faulty).

2. The Outputs must be consistent and actually reflect the activity or performance that is being measured. Most metrics are a measurement of Input compared to Output.

3. The Method of Measurement needs to be one where the data is relatively easy to collect and does not need to be manipulated or adjusted in order to make it meaningful.

4. Before you collect a specific metric, you must have determined what the measurement of it means in terms of desired performance. If the metric is quality-based then the definitions of the varying qualities must be predefined. If the metric is quantity-based then the targets or minimums and maximums must be established to ensure that performance is improving.

5. In order to make metric measuring a value added activity, there must be some target, standard, or budget set to the metric so that the person monitoring the metric can quickly assess whether things are going well or not.

6. While not always possible, the best metrics will tell the reader why the performance or activity is not going as it should.

## CLASSES OF PERFORMANCE MEASURES

### *Productivity-Based*

These metrics are the simplest to set because they are relatively easy to account for and most often used to determine whether someone is being productive, which we hope translates to being effective. An example is the measurement of the average time it takes for an employee to make collection calls compared to the number of delinquent customers they actually contacted.

### *Achievement-Based*

These metrics are relatively easy to establish because they are usually time driven. Examples include closing the general ledger by the second working day or having all the accounts payable vouchers posted by 4:00 PM on Friday.

### *Composition-Based*

These metrics can be described as how many pieces exist and are used for comparing one person's performance against the total. For example, you divide the entire vendor list alphabetically among your three Accounts Payable Specialists: Perry, Merry and Kerry. Perry works with the vendors from the letter A through D, which constitutes 33 percent of your payable activity. Merry has vendors from the letter E through M, which constitutes 42 percent of your payable activity. Kerry handles vendors N through Z, which constitutes 25 percent of all vendor activity. You can compare this metric against the number of invoices each person entered for the month.

## RIGHT METRIC MIX

Depending upon your goals and the critical performance you need to measure, you will select the appropriate performance measures. In public accounting, for example, the majority of the metrics we use to measure employee performance are productivity-based. In internal accounting, the majority of the metrics we track are productivity-based and achievement-based.

### *Metrics—Objective vs. Subjective*

The best type of metric is objective in nature. This means that they cannot be manipulated or swayed by emotional issues or judgment calls. It may not always be possible for you to have a complete set of metrics that are always objective. Some of the metrics in your scorecard will end up being the subjective kind, those that are subject to a person's judgment.

You can create conditions so the metrics that fall into the subjective category will not be used to cover up problems or present things in the best possible light. An example of such a metric is your firm's safety record. By defining upfront exactly what constitutes a reportable safety issue and by having a methodology to ensure that every injury is reported, you help to remove the subjectivity out of that particular metric.

Another thing that you can do to make a subjective metric reliable is to conduct an occasional audit of the data and its collection process to ensure that people are not biasing the input or spinning the output. Using the same example of your safety record, obtaining independent information from supervisors and from employees about injuries would prevent the two groups from colluding to keep your firm's safety record high.

If you really think about it, almost every metric has a subjective component. Therefore, to ensure that metrics measure the important things and that they are used to make smarter decisions, your emphasis on training employees about metrics is to help them understand the value of each metric. This includes training on not only how to collect the data, but how the metric is used and the decisions that stem from each metric. During training, the firm's leaders need to talk about good decision-making and the consequences of poor decision-making.

Over time, with experience in collecting, reporting, and fine-tuning the metrics that you use to measure business activities, you will find numerous ways to turn in each metric from subjective to objective. Again there is nothing wrong with having subjective metrics in your firm's or client's scorecard. The concern about subjective metrics needs to be on whether or not employees can manipulate the data or present the information in ways that undermines the honest feedback that you are attempting to collect.

MAKING PERFORMANCE MEASURES WORK

These suggestions will help you gain the full benefits of performance measuring.

- When using soft data, be sure that there is no incentive to invent or add a positive spin to the data.

- Help managers find the weaknesses and identify failures of their existing performance measures.

- Use the 80/20 rule in designing and reporting on performance measures.

- Identify the fewest activities that have the greatest impact on stakeholder value.

- Combine financial and nonfinancial measures together for a single metric.

## *Categories and Examples of Performance Measures*

The following are categories of performance measures, including examples for each category.

### *Environmental Indicators*

- Safety record

- Pollution prevention efforts

*Market and Customer Indicators*

- Market penetration

- Share of wallet

*Competition Indicators*

- Speed to market

- Percentage of revenue from new products

*Internal Business Process Indicators*

- Defect analysis

- Capacity utilization

*Human Resource Indicators*

- Employee morale level

- Employee satisfaction

*Financial Indicators*

- Economic Value Added rate (see chapter 2)

- Activity-based product costs

## Tactic 4: Help Them Fly in Formation

**"In our factory, we make lipstick. In our advertising, we sell hope."**

**Charles Revson, chairman of Revlon**

Have you ever watched a flock of geese flying? Each goose knows its role and what is expected of it, so that the flock reaches its destination. You will be successful as a Hired Gun when you assist your clients to fly in disciplined formation like the geese.

### *Hired Gun Tool: Critical Success Factor*

The purpose of this best practice is to ensure that you understand how the company's most important performance is directly connected to the profits and to the employee's day-to-day decisions and actions. Except in small companies or professional service organizations, rarely does the average employee understand how his role fits into the big picture of what the organization is all about. Yet, studies have shown that when employees understand how their role fits into the scheme of the business model, they become more effective, remain loyal, and stay accountable.

**The purpose of the client's Critical Success Factor is to be an early warning system!**

In this best practice you will discover that you can connect the most crucial strategy to people's day-to-day actions. Better yet, you will be able to improve reporting on what is important and what is important to measure.

Let us deepen your understanding of this best practice by going into some key terminology.

STRATEGY DEFINED

Strategy is a hypothesis about cause and effect. This hypothesis says, "If we do this then our customers will pay us this." For example, Starbucks' hypothesis is: "If we make coffee snobs of our customers they will pay premium prices for our products!" Their strategy or hypothesis works.

Boeing had a hypothesis that was "If we make jets that are reliable, safe, and fuel efficient our customers will pay premium prices for our jets." That worked for a while until Airbus found a way to make safe, reliable, and fuel efficient jets at a cost less than Boeing's.** Boeing's theory fell apart because they omitted from their strategy: "Listen to the customer!" Boeing's leaders have been working hard since the early 90s to recover from this oversight. (** Ignore any heartache you have about how several European governments may be subsidizing Airbus and hiding the true cost of making jets!)

Your client's (firm's) strategy is a theory and only remains one until it is proven that you can execute your strategy. This is why the Controller's feedback is so critical in making a business model successful and sustainable. Your feedback, if focused on the strategy, tells your client's executive team whether or not they are able to apply their theory of cause and effect successfully.

ORGANIZATIONAL ALIGNMENT DEFINED

Organizational alignment is when all the elements of an organization work together in concert within the company's ideology (see Strategy) and the type of success it intends to achieve.

CRITICAL SUCCESS FACTOR DEFINED

A company's Critical Success Factor is a strategy or uniqueness that defines the most important performance of a business because it determines your success or failure.

The Critical Success Factor answers this question: "What do we need to do in our business to differentiate ourselves from our direct competitor?"

Your Critical Success Factor is the highest level performance measurement.

**Examples**

Starbucks' Critical Success Factor is making coffee snobs of their customers.

McDonald's Critical Success Factor is consistency and value of their products.

Microsoft has a Critical Success Factor of integration of their software product family.

Boeing's Critical Success Factor is the safety, reliability, and fuel efficiency of their jets.

Wal-Mart's Critical Success Factor can be defined as constantly streamlining distribution so that their product's selling price is lower than anybody else's.

Costco differentiates itself from Wal-Mart by having a Critical Success Factor of focusing on their customer and providing a smaller range of products and services at consistently low prices.

It is incumbent upon the Controller and CFO to isolate their client's (employer's) Critical Success Factor. If the leaders of the organization are smart and business savvy they already know what that factor is and can explain it. If they do not, give each leader the Howard Hughes Test to find out how they measure the success or failure of their business.

PERFORMANCE DRIVERS THAT COULD BE CRITICAL SUCCESS FACTORS

Performance drivers that could be Critical Success Factors include

- Surveys of your competition's prices

- Investments in innovations or new technology

- Portfolio of assets

- Number of customized offerings

- Internal capacity

- Lower than average product or distribution costs

- Lower than average product development time

- Targeted marketing mailings results

## Performance Measuring Principle

**We are all in the information business!**

The Controller or CFO's responsibility is to develop a reporting system that contains a series of integrated performance metrics which measure if the Critical Success Factor is being achieved and the business plan is being executed. To be successful in reporting faster, the Controller must concentrate on reporting metrics instead of historical financial data.

## Drivers of an "Information Business"

Even if your client (employer) does not do business in a worldwide arena, you still need to be aware of what is driving successful businesses today. Though you may work for a typical mom-and-pop small business, your customers are constantly being lured away by a variety of means, such as the Internet, and by large firms who may not currently provide what you do, but are looking for ways to get into your marketplace.

From a big-picture perspective, these are the drivers of successful business organizations, such as Wal-Mart and Cisco Systems, to name a few. Notice how each one relies on having timely and insightful information to stay on top of this business driver, including

- Cross-function and integration so the firm can provide more services and one stop solutions for customers

- Links to customers and suppliers for instantaneous trend analysis

- Customer segmentations to tailor solutions across specific target markets

- Doing business on a global scale for economic reasons, like outsourcing tax preparation and customer service to India

- Innovation

- Knowledge workers

> **Answer This Question**
>
> Where, on a typical GAAP financial statement, would you find feedback if the firm was being successful in managing these key Business Drivers?

**Your traditional financial statements *do not* provide feedback on the drivers of today's Information Business!**

## AVOID THE CONTROLLER KISS OF DEATH

To anyone with more than three years of experience in the Controller or CFO position, the answer is obvious: "You cannot find feedback anywhere on a GAAP financial statement for these drivers!"

I gave you the self-test to remind those who are still using GAAP financial statements as the cornerstone of your Controller's reports that you are not *thinking strategically*! From my informal surveys of Controllers across the United States and Canada, I estimate that between 25 percent to 35 percent are still using GAAP-based reports, such as the accrual Income Statement, the Balance Sheet, and the Cash Flows as the main internal reports that you issue to executives.

I am not saying that Income Statement and Statement of Cash Flows are unimportant. They are important only to external users, such as your bank and any sophisticated investor. The reports that executives and others inside your firm rely on most are those that are operationally oriented. CEOs rarely ask how much money you have tied up in receivables and inventories before making an operating decision. They want information such as daily production rates and orders received, number of quotes issued, and number of website hits to run the business.

This means that you must tailor your reports to what they are looking for in the way of feedback regarding the execution of their business plans. If you fail to do this, you will soon find that you will be replaced, or they will turn to and rely on other databases of information that do not reside in accounting. If people in your organization do this, it is known as the Controller's Kiss of Death. Your data from the GL becomes subject to question and considered invalid or irrelevant.

Our responsibility to our client (employer) is to develop a reporting system that contains a series of integrated performance metrics, which measures if the Critical Success Factor is being achieved. This reporting system also tells you whether the firm is accomplishing the strategies that are driving your business model. Notice that to be successful in this the Controller must really understand how the business model works and understand the sales and delivery process from the outside in.

## Tactic 5: Keep Your Eyes on the Forest

**Never sweat the petty things. Never pet the sweaty things.**

### *Daily Prioritization and Calibration*

Controllers, accountants, and financial people tend to be detail-oriented (otherwise, we would not have accomplished as much as we have). However, sticking to the details is a downfall of the part-time or contract Controller. To be successful, you must start each day focusing on the forest, or you will get lost in the trees.

**As the solution-maker, you cannot afford to get slowed down in the minutiae that employees deal with every day.**

If your only experience has been as a consultant (that is, CPA firm employee) this may seem obvious. If you have recently been in an organization as a full-time employee, it is very easy to lose sight of the forest for the trees. This is where the skills of staying focused, establishing priorities, and sticking to your vision benefit you. These are covered in chapter 6.

---

**Answer This Question**

How do you keep your focus on the forest in your current job?

---

WHY YOU MUST STAY OUT OF THE DAY-TO-DAY MINUTIAE

As I stated in chapter 4 on the attitudes of the Hired Gun, except for the person who has been a consultant for many years, the typical contract Controller started in a full-time employee capacity. Just as it is dangerous to be emotionally involved with the client, it is deadly to become involved in the day-to-day stuff that happens in every workplace. Besides a multitude of employee meetings, there are office parties, water cooler chats, sports pools, and so on.

Each day there is a tremendous amount of time and energy spent in every organization that is not necessarily productive or beneficial to the ultimate customer. Once, I was asked to help in a search for a critical missing file. My entire accounting team spent three hours searching for it. As a Hired Gun, you cannot afford to waste valuable time on things like this.

Before becoming involved in anything, just stop and ask yourself this question: "Will this activity move me a step closer to helping the client or will it provide me information that will make me invaluable?"

If the answer is an obvious "No," then do not get involved with it. Over time, identifying these non-value adding activities will become easier to spot and easier to avoid.

The following are specific techniques to practice each day, which will enable you to stay out of the minutiae, as you work to solve the client's problems.

This skill goes hand in glove with the skill of focus, which is covered in chapter 6.

WAYS TO SEE THE FOREST

Tips for avoiding getting bogged down in minutiae include:

- Plan, plan, plan, plan, and plan some more.

- Keep your supervision responsibilities to a minimum.

- Establish employee teams to take on major responsibilities.

- Hold frequent short meetings designed to accomplish things without the responsibility of leading them.

- Delegate as much as you dare and then delegate even more.

- Empower employees to make decisions and solve their own problems.

- Keep track of where and how you spend your time.

- Schedule and use quiet time to think and dream.

- Rely on other people's abilities and creativity.

- Think strategically.

- Think holistically.

- Develop deep trust (covered in Skill of Leadership).

*Plan, Plan, Plan, Plan, and Plan Some More*

Each day that you work for the client, go in with a specific plan. Before ending your day (or time) with the client, make notes on what you need to do next. Plan not just for tomorrow but for two to three weeks from today.

*Keep Your Supervision Responsibilities to a Minimum*

Unless you are a part-time Controller, exclude yourself from taking on full supervisory responsibilities. This may be hard to do if you are filling in for an incumbent Controller or CFO. In a later chapter, there will be suggestions on how to do this in the section called Creating Opportunities for Others. In a nutshell, find seasoned employees who are able to take over critical supervisory responsibilities, so that you can spend your time on important things.

*Establish a Team to Take on Major Responsibilities*

One of the best ways you can serve your client is to take the accounting department and mold it into a real team. Today in accounting, a true team consists of generalists who can take on multiple roles. A talented generalist has the ability to do payroll one day and accounts payable the next. In addition, one of the traits of an effective team is the ability to make sure the work gets done, even when someone is absent or the work is not evenly distributed. This way of adding value to a client may not be possible in a short-term project. At least consider doing what you can to turn the accounting group from a department mentality into a team mindset.

***Hold Frequent Short Meetings Designed to Accomplish Things Without the Responsibility of Leading Them***

If you are serving as the Controller and you have work to get done through others, you will be required to hold staff meetings. It is likely you will be in meetings with other company managers. At the outset, inform your client that you will be absent from any meeting that does not have a specific agenda and defined outcomes. For those meetings that you attend, schedule your time so that you are only in attendance for the agenda items that require you to be there.

You do not have to be present at every meeting, but instead can send one of your employees to take notes for you and keep you informed about what went on. In addition, you can submit formal reports that can be summarized by one of your staff. Running meetings is a responsibility that can be turned into an opportunity for another employee.

***Delegate as Much as You Dare and Then Delegate Even More***

Chapter 6 offers suggestions on how you can accomplish this. Just make sure that you go into each project with the intention of delegating much of the daily work to others, so that you can focus on what the client expects you to accomplish.

***Empower Employees to Make Decisions and Solve Their Own Problems***

Since you will not be around 100 percent of the time, one of the most important things you can do to help an accounting department succeed is to empower employees to make their own decisions and solve their own problems. Just like establishing a team attitude, this takes time. Go into each project with the determination to move decision-making in accounting down to the lowest level possible.

A recommended strategy many Hired Guns adopt is to require that anyone who comes to you with a problem also brings you three suggested solutions. Unless the person fails to have thought through possible solutions, they cannot spend time with you until they do. From personal experience I find that, whenever I turn away people without solutions, only 40 percent of them will return for assistance and 99 percent of these will have a viable solution. The other 60 percent do not return because either they solved the problem themselves or realized that they did not have a problem in the first place.

***Keep Track of Where and How You Spend Your Time***

If you are not in public accounting, this may feel like a step backwards. However, this is very critical to your success in a contractor or consultant capacity. You must get in the habit of keeping track of your time. Keeping a log or timesheet is much more than a billing issue. For example, the client is expecting you to decrease the length of time it takes to collect receivables and improve the effectiveness of the collection calls. Keeping track of the amount of time you spend on this project will help you to determine if you are spinning your wheels or not dedicating enough time for this outcome.

From a revenue standpoint you need to also know how much free time you are giving away to your client so that you can factor that into your rate structure or to bid your next project better.

*Schedule and Use Quiet Time to Think and Dream*

At first this may sound funny but let me continue…

Imagine someone you work with is sitting at a desk staring out the window looking at the beautiful sky. As you walk by their office and notice this, your first thought is, "Marley certainly does not have enough work to do!" *Wrong!*

We Controllers and CFOs spend far too much time doing and not enough time thinking or dreaming. We fear someone saying about us—"He or she is wasting time or does not have enough to do."

The more time you spend quietly dreaming and thinking, the more effective you become. It is difficult to be creative when you are busy racing the clock.

Allow yourself permission to take between 30 to 45 minutes each day to sit in a quiet place to dream and think. Remember to have a pad of paper and pencil or your laptop handy to write down all the great ideas that come from your quiet time.

*Rely on Other People's Abilities and Creativity*

Most of the employees that you will work with have a tremendous amount of ability and creativity even if they do not show it to you. Part of your role as the Hired Gun is to create the opportunity for others to shine. Try informing someone, in a sincere and humble way, that you require their assistance. You will be amazed at how much people are willing to help you.

Even though the client has hired you—the expert—to solve their issue, you are not doing this alone. You must rely on others.

*Think Strategically and Holistically*

Whenever wearing the hat of solution creator, keep the following in mind:

- The Hired Gun's initial goal is to uncover the client's pain.

- The Hired Gun's ultimate goal is to build a relationship of trust.

- The Hired Gun treats each person as a client in order to maintain a professional approach to problem solving.

- The Hired Gun's professional demeanor helps find realistic and innovative solutions for the client.

- The Hired Gun's professional demeanor helps build a relationship of trust with those who rely on the Hired Gun's acumen and insight.

- The Hired Gun strives to be an equal partner with the client because a partnership means that each party is invested in the relationship.

- The client rarely knows what the source of their pain is because they are too close to the action to see things objectively. This is where the Hired Gun becomes invaluable.

Your most valuable tools for uncovering the client's pain are

- GAP Analysis (see chapter 7).

- Probing Questions (see the Appendix).

## Conclusion

This chapter highlighted five key tools that every contract accounting professional will need to have in their own toolkit. Starting with a Position Description, you (the contract Controller) can use this tool to help define the areas of responsibility you agree to accept and come to terms with what the client expects from you.

The second tool used to define what is important will benefit you in numerous ways. You can only have a satisfied client when you deliver what they expect and understand their needs from the inside out.

The third tool, performance metrics, will serve you in many ways. By helping your client (your employer) to measure the right activities, you will assist them in driving the appropriate behaviors that lead to lasting profitability and success.

Once you understand the correct set of performance metrics to build a viable scorecard, the next logical step is to apply the tool of defining the client's Critical Success Factor. This factor is the most important and high-level metric that defines what the business is about. As an objective observer, you are in an excellent position to help the client define and then capitalize on their unique Critical Success Factor.

The last tool is crucial to your long-term success as a Hired Gun, which is to remember the forest. As accountants, it is very easy to get so focused on the task at hand that you lose sight of the big picture. As a consultant and person only devoting a limited number of hours to each client, you must be able to constantly look at the bigger picture for the benefit of yourself and of your client.

# Chapter 6

# Hired Gun Skills—Part 1

**"The trouble with being a leader in a dysfunctional company is that you can't tell if the employees are following you or chasing you."**

**Ron Rael, Leadership Coach**

## Introduction

After completing this chapter you should be able to

- Apply the skill of focus to be more productive.

- Increase your ability to lead by articulating your vision and creating opportunities for others.

- Enhance accountability, including your own.

- Improve how you communicate.

- Name and strengthen the three Controller's Building Blocks.

- Get results from better priority management.

## Daily Skill Set that Benefits the Client

In this chapter, we will concentrate on four specific skills that a part-time and contract Controller will need to be successful. While the technical, number crunching, and analytical skills are very important, we will assume you already have them. This particular skill set has both a technical and a softer side. For example, leadership includes accountability, communication, creating opportunities, and visioning.

Yet, to help the clients you serve, you often need to combine your financial acumen with your leadership abilities. It is a rare project where a Hired Gun can devote every client hour to number crunching or spreadsheet building. You will be involved with people and working with people to get things accomplished 99 percent of the time. Please do not dismiss the importance of these four valuable skills.

## Special Skills the Hired Gun Uses Daily

The four special skills the Hired Gun uses daily include

- Focus

- Systems Building

- Priority Management

- Leadership

  **Because accountability cannot be delegated, it takes a leap of faith for the leader to trust that others not only have the capacity to step up but also have the commitment to make whatever contribution is required. You must be willing to live with the results they create!**

---

**Activity 6-1: Perils of Pauline, Part 6**

When you worked as Pauline's supervisor in public accounting, you noticed that she had a difficult time getting her work done within the hours budgeted.

Regarding the skill of priority management, what advice can you give her about the position she is considering?

---

In 2005, nine top-tier companies had temporary CEOs. The study, conducted by public relations firm Weber Shandwick attributes this rise to a usually high CEO turnover and an increased willingness for board of directors to fire lackluster CEOs before finding a permanent replacement. Most temporary CEOs outperformed their permanent peers.

---

Siegfried Group is a CPA firm in Philadelphia that launched a unit to provide skilled people to Fortune 1,000 companies for major interim projects that require intensive high-level financial services. This unit is the fastest growing part of their practice.

Rob Siegfried, Founder and CEO of the Siegfried Group, said:

"We are not taking over any functions for a client, but are instead giving them the talented people to take extra work on themselves. We provide high caliber financial professionals to [clients] when they have responsibilities that are greater than the existing resources can handle." Besides one-time-only projects, they provide talent for regularly scheduled crunch times such as year-end closing.

# Skill #1: Focus

**"Through focused efforts miracles are performed."**
**Ron Rael, Leadership Coach**

---

**Answer This Question**

Imagine that you have a pile of work in front of you on your desk, and it is Thursday morning. You leave for a long vacation on Friday at 6 p.m.

What do you do to get out of the office with a clear conscience?

---

**You become very focused!**

## *Focus*

You probably prevent distractions, allocate your time, and do only those things that are important. Doing this is part of the skill of focus. Being focused is being productive. This skill, however, is one the part-time or contract Controller needs every day, not just when facing a tight deadline.

There is a real difference between being busy and being productive. There is also a clear distinction between being effective and productive. We are so very busy that we forget the differences.

## PRODUCTIVITY DEFINED

Productivity is putting in effort so that the result exceeds the effort. Being productive can be being efficient but being efficient is not always being productive.

Imagine that you spend three hours trying to track down a 5¢ error in the general ledger. Are you being productive? You already know the answer: you definitely are not. Why? Because your effort far exceeded the result (in this case, identifying a minor error).

This seems obvious, yet every month I meet a Controller whose boss, the CEO, the President, or worse, the CFO, requires that person to look for any discrepancies and book every entry no matter how immaterial.

While this might work if you are the full-time Controller for your employer, you will soon find yourself out of a job if you do this as the contract Controller. Your goal is to be productive at least 90 percent of the time while you are working on each client project.

## EFFICIENCY DEFINED

Efficiency is dotting all the I's and crossing all the T's. All accounting work is an exacting science, meaning that we try for accuracy and strive for efficiency. All too many accountants focus on efficiency instead of productivity. When someone is being anal to the point where they are being unproductive, apply the rule of 80/20. Eighty percent of the time you can achieve your goal by getting something done quickly without striving for 100 percent accuracy.

Accountants are so afraid of being wrong, that they would rather be 100 percent right than 10 percent wrong. This makes you both inefficient and unproductive.

The main difference between productivity and efficiency is doing the right things instead of doing things right! As Tom Peters reminds his clients, there were many efficient buggy whip suppliers, but they went out of business because they missed what was happening in the transportation industry.

## WAYS TO STAY FOCUSED AND BE PRODUCTIVE

Ways to stay focused and be productive include

- Have clear-cut goals.

- Know what is important.

- Set priorities and stick to them.

- Be excellent in priority management.

### Having Clear-Cut Goals

About half the people who work in accounting are goal machines. Once these folks have set a goal, they will achieve it. It is important that you know which 50 percent group you are in. To be successful as a Hired Gun, you must have specific clear goals and be able to execute most of them. More information will be covered on completing your goals in chapter 7.

### Knowing What Is Important

This was highlighted in chapter 5 but bears repeating. In order to be productive and focused, you must start out by knowing what is important to your client. You might think getting your files in order is important, but it detracts you from making the improvements your client expects you to make.

This is why communication with your client on a weekly basis is beneficial to you as the contract Controller. With weekly status reports and discussions, you can identify what is important to your client so that you can hone in on that area. This also helps if the client's priority shifts during your engagement.

### Setting Priorities and Sticking to Them

People who are productive do so by spending time defining the priority for the day or for the hour, and then not allowing anything to interrupt them from that priority. If you only have one client this may be rather easy to do. However, most Hired Guns have between three and five client projects going at any one time. Therefore to stay productive, setting and sticking to priorities is extremely critical because you cannot afford to let any one project action item fall through the cracks.

*Being Excellent in Priority Management*

You probably have taken a class or seminar on time management. However, time management is outdated. In today's online, real-time, 24/7, fast-paced world, the emphasis is on priority management. The priorities you set determine and drive how and where you spend your time. This is better explained in Skill #3.

Here is a motto that I keep at my desk and have committed to memory. Make it your motto! At the end the day and week, ask yourself

**With the time I had available, did I accomplish my goals in priority order?**

If you can answer yes most of the time, you will be very successful as a Hired Gun.

---

**Answer These Questions**

How can the skill of focus benefit the part-time Controller?

How can the skill of focus benefit the contract Controller?

---

## Skill #2: Systems Building

**A bad system will defeat a great performance 9 out of 10 times.**

People who are currently successful as a contract or part-time Controller use a systems approach to doing their jobs.

---

**Answer This Question**

What is a systems approach?

---

### Systems Approach to Accounting

A systems approach is envisioning the whole process from end-result back to the beginning. In a systems approach, you design the methodology to ensure you deliver what is expected.

The Controller's area of responsibility consists of three interconnected systems or building blocks. By developing a support system in each block, you will be able to stay on top of whatever comes your way.

THE WISE CONTROLLER'S SYSTEMS

The three systems shown in figure 6-1 integrate with each other, but the last two rely heavily on the one below it. You cannot run an accounting department unless you have people. So you develop a people system. Then you need to plan the work of those folks, so you develop a planning system. To make sure the work gets done, develop a system for communicating with one another.

**Figure 6-1: Controller's Building Blocks**

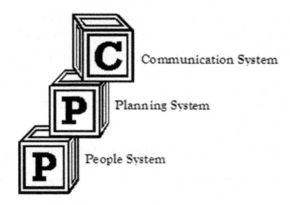

## Base Block—Controller's People Systems

We will not cover the entire items that could fall under your people systems. Unless you are a Hired Gun who specializes in the human resource area, most of your focus on the people systems of your client will be to make sure that employees work together and get the job done to your satisfaction. For this building block, we will concentrate on the universal tool for solving people problems: *feedback.*

**The problem:** People will always create their own answers in the absence of information and they will almost always think the worst.

**The solution:** Spend at least an hour each day giving and receiving feedback.

> "Feedback is the process of sharing information with another person for the purpose of reinforcing or changing her or his behavior. By providing clear feedback, the [Leader] builds trust, removes interpersonal barriers, and guides others towards improved performance."
>
> *Essential Facilitation*, Interaction Associates

### *What Feedback Is and Is Not*

Feedback is the truth about you, as I (your supervisor) see it. From the employee's point of view, feedback means the difference between being in the dark and knowing where I stand. Your feedback allows me to see if I am who I believe myself to be. It provides me with tangible information on how I am doing. Feedback is the favorite tool of successful supervisors, because it creates two-way dialogue with the employee.

If feedback is driven by fear, it will be avoided and few of the facts will be received. This occurs when the employee has done something incorrectly and is afraid you are about to lay down the hammer. To be an effective supervisor, you must get in the habit of giving feedback when the employee does things right. All too frequently, we ignore all the positive actions and decisions and only give feedback when the employee errs. Feedback is not criticism. This is exactly what you are giving when you only notice the incorrect behaviors and do not comment on the correct ones.

Feedback can have a strong impact on motivation when the employee expects to receive it immediately. Feedback is best used when it is given daily, because daily doses of feedback will maintain the high performance level of your star performers. People want, crave, and desire feedback. Feedback taps into our human motivators of accomplishment and inner satisfaction.

What happens when feedback is absent? In the absence of specific feedback, people invent their own performance standards. The only time people know what you are thinking is when you tell them. Silence leaves employees trying to figure out what is on your mind, and 99.9 percent of the time they are wrong.

## WHAT FEEDBACK DOES

Feedback does the following

- Honors competence and reinforces behavior

- Helps align expectations and priorities

- Fills gaps in people's knowledge

- Lets employees know areas to correct

- Alleviates fear of the unknown

- Fosters open communication

- Builds trust

- Rewards top performers

- Creates a consequence for poor performers

- Sets up expectations and standards

- Creates a professional atmosphere

- Improves interdependence

## HOW LEADERS USE FEEDBACK

Leaders use feedback in the following ways:

- They just do it.

- They use it to change unacceptable behavior.

- They use it to reinforce positive behavior.

- They give feedback frequently and intimately.

- They focus it on service to the customer.

- They find ways around the system if the culture does not value feedback.

- They first build a foundation with the person.

- They understand the difference between judging and describing.

## HOW TO KEEP FEEDBACK OBJECTIVE

Another reason people fear feedback is because the person giving it does not understand the difference between judging and describing. A lot of the feedback is purely a judgment call on the giver's part. Your goal as a supervisor and team leader is to identify those behaviors that you want repeated and those behaviors that you want altered or improved. This means that you must be able to clearly describe the specific behavior to the employee and explain the positive or negative aspects of the behavior without any biases. Table 6-1 illustrates an example of the difference between judging and describing.

**Table 6-1: Difference between Judging and Describing**

| "I do not think you have the right attitude." | This is a judgment statement by you based on your beliefs or biases. |
|---|---|
| "I saw you ignore Tom's request for help. Your job requires that you support Tom in his work." | This is a describing statement explaining what you objectively observed without expressing an opinion. |

## WHEN AND WHERE TO USE FEEDBACK

Feedback does not begin the moment an employee does something wrong. It commences the day the employee starts working for you. The more you can provide feedback in the early stages of an employee's employment, the quicker you will shorten their learning curve and mold the employee into the star performer you believe they can be. In addition to orientation and training, the following are the areas where it is critical for you as a leader and supervisor to provide ongoing and supportive feedback:

- Orienting and training new employees

- Teaching a new set of job skills

- Explaining the standards of the department or team

- Explaining the cultural norms or political realities

- Correcting performance

- Changing goals or business conditions

- Adjusting to a new team

- Assisting employees in unfamiliar work experiences

- Helping new employees set priorities

- Following up on an important training session

- Dealing with an employee with declining performance

- Reinforcing good performance

- Encouraging superior performance

- Performing an informal performance review

- Preparing employees to meet their future career goals

- Preparing employees for more challenging work assignments

- Building an employee's self-confidence

- Providing an emotional pick-me-up for an employee

- Dealing with power battles that harm the team's cohesiveness

## 2nd Block—Controller's Planning System

As stated many times in this book, your client will place high expectations on you to get the work done quickly. Your planning system for the accounting department or team must work to ensure that you can meet those expectations and obligations. This building block especially covers how you plan the work and ensure that the deadlines will be met.

As a Hired Gun and professional, you will have your own methodology for doing this. When called to clean up the mess, you may find the accounting team does not have a methodology for keeping track of its workflow or for ensuring that deadlines are met. This may be an area where you can add value to your client by creating such a system.

Many contract Controllers find that putting together systems, processes, and checklists have made a huge difference for their clients. If you are just starting out as a contract Controller, think about what has made you successful in meeting deadlines and discharging your obligations. Then compare what your client's employees use with what you use.

### What Every Employee Wants to Know

Besides tools for planning the work, do not forget that employees have questions about where you and the team are headed. The following is a checklist to remind you to keep the members of your accounting team informed about such things:

- Where is the organization heading?

- How will it get there?

- What are the issues?

- Is management prepared to resolve the problems?

- What does it all mean to me?

- Who can I turn to for the real information?

## 3rd Block—Controller's Communication System

**Leadership is communication.**

**To manage well, we need to communicate well.**

### *Hired Gun Credibility Comes from Great Communication*

As I have stated many times before, your project for the client will most likely include working with and through other people. Therefore, communication takes on a whole new level of responsibility when you are the contract Controller.

The third Controller's Building Block is the communication system. Since most of your projects will run between three and nine months, you will not be able to fix every communication roadblock or deficiency. However, go into each project with an awareness that the core of 97 percent of all business problems stems from a lack of communication.

Knowing this fact gives you an opportunity to have a quick impact by making some quick fixes in the accounting department's system of communication. This section contains a few checklists and reminders about what it takes to be seen as a competent communicator. We will start with five rules about communication in a typical organization.

RULES OF ORGANIZATIONAL COMMUNICATION

Five rules of organization communication are as follows:

1. Good communication is impossible without leaders consistently doing the right thing, according to the needs of the problem or situation, to the best of their ability.

2. Employees of an organization do not inherently identify their own interests with the interests of the organization. No matter how well or poorly the organization is doing, employees sometimes have difficulty seeing what stake they have in it.

3. Employees have multiple sources of information. They are not chiefly dependent on what they are told through official channels. The employees' most trusted information is their own day-to-day experiences.

4. Do not ask for an employee's opinion or suggestions unless you really care and intend to act upon that information.

5. When any negative event occurs which leads to employee rage, no matter the source or cause, the anger will manifest itself. Employees who feel wronged will find a way to express their feelings, to the detriment of the organization.

### *Hired Gun Tool: Communication Web*

A communication web is the key to staying informed and keeping others appraised of what is going on.

## CREATE YOUR OWN COMMUNICATION WEB

Put an image of a large spider's web into your mind. Notice how it is woven. Notice how it sticks to everything. Notice that although it is soft, it has a daunting strength. Notice finally how hard it is to get rid of.

Next, think about a website that you enjoy visiting. What features does it have that you admire? Most good websites have great features. They are/have

- Interactive.

- Easy to navigate.

- Built with redundancies through links.

- Available 24/7.

- Fast loading.

- Just the right amount of information.

- A query or navigation box.

- A one-click feature so you can communicate with whom you need.

- Transaction verification.

- A one-click feature so you can receive communication back from the site.

- Designed so you can find what you need quickly.

*What does this mean?*

With the pace of business and the other factors that make workplace communication challenging, we need a new model to use in order to make sure effective communication keeps up with the pace of business.

This new model is a Communication Web, a concept developed by Kelly Catlin Walker.

Your project team or department's approach for communicating needs to be a system that contains the best features of a website and a spider web.

## FEATURES OF A COMMUNICATION WEB

A communication structure built around the web concept has these specific features:

- People have access to information and data 24/7.

- Everyone has multiple points of contact.

- Information is thoughtfully archived.

- Information is easily accessible.

- Information is easy to find.

- Redundancies are installed to ensure that any communication gaps or blockages do not prevent people from being in the loop.

- The structure is flexible yet strong.

- People verify that their communication was received and understood.

- The web itself is under constant development and improvement.

- With ease, just like the one-click feature, everyone can be reached by one e-mail or one phone call.

- No one person is flooded with information.

- No one person is inaccessible.

- No one person is the bottleneck for the flow of communication.

The most important feature is that whether a person is present or not, everyone stays connected to the web of information.

## *How to Design a Communication Web*

Most communication webs are built around multiple communication platforms. They include hardware, software, and protocols that

- Transmit data electronically.

- Archive key data like meeting notes for easy retrieval.

- Digitize information quickly so it is accessible by all.

- Has a calendar that is shared by everyone.

- Has a priority structure for e-mails that everyone abides by; for example,

  - Priority 1—urgent or critical.

  - Priority 2—important.

  - Priority 3—some importance.

  - Priority 4—FYI only.

- Ensures every customer (internal and external) has multiple points of contacts.

- Guarantees information is disseminated easily without the need for frequent face-to-face meetings.

- Provides regular diagnosis and checking to improve the flow of communication.

- Identifies ways of getting information so that if one system fails, people are still in the loop; for example,

  - E-mail.

  - Voice mail.

  - Memos.

  - Electronic file sharing.

  - Internet postings.

  - Electronic bulletin boards.

  - Status reports.

  - Wall charts.

- Finally, everyone's priority #1 is to keep communication flowing.

## COMMUNICATION WEB KEY DECISIONS

Key decisions that need to be made when designing a communication web include

- Who prepares the agenda?

- How are the suggestions to the agenda handled?

- Who maintains the action items or project lists?

- Who coordinates among the team members?

- Who keeps the other teams informed?

- Who communicates to non-members involved with us?

- Who updates members unable to attend the meeting?

- How will the information best be communicated?

- How do we ensure members read the communications?

- How do we ensure everyone with a need to know is included?

- How are issues and disagreements raised?

## COMMUNICATION WEB IMPACT ZONES

The tool, shown in figure 6-2, is designed to ensure that everyone whom a change affects is consulted and informed.

**Figure 6-2: Communication Impact Zones**

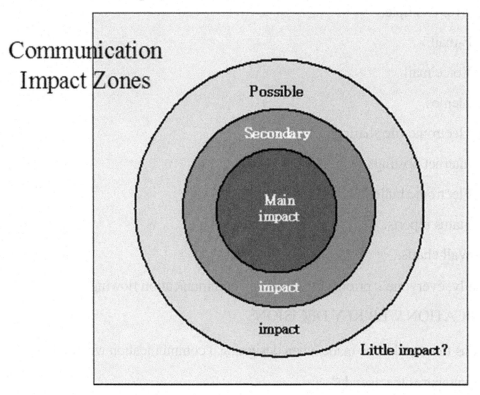

> **"We the uniformed, working for the inaccessible, are doing the impossible for the ungrateful!"**
> **Employee's lament**

This tool reduces the likelihood of receiving these common and valid complaints from employees:

- I was blindsided by the change!

- No one took into consideration the impact of the change on my job!

- This change may have solved the problem, but it created four more!

COMMUNICATION WEB FOUNDATION FOR RECEPTIVE COMMUNICATION

When these take place, employees will be willing to give something of themselves back to the company.

- Help the employee master their job.

- Create a predictable work environment.

- Value employees as people (remember: they want to be loved!).

*Communication Web Necessities for a Completed Communication*

Every good communication system has four elements to ensure that the actual message has been carried. These apply for one-on-one conversations, as well as in team interactions.

1. *Delivery*—The act of making the communication clear and visible.

2. *Receiving*—The act of hearing and understanding the message.

3. *Feedback*—Taking the time to check to confirm that the message was received and understood.

4. *Monitoring*—Taking the time to check back later to see if the message has been acted upon and has remained the same.

## Hired Gun Tool: Communication Web System Checklist

See how many of these apply to your employer or client. See how many apply to the team you lead or are a member of.

___Your company has good communication! It is the process that is being neglected.

**Solution:** Your organization is defined by how well it communicates internally.

___A majority of communications end without any kind of summary of what was covered or agreed to.

**Solution:** When parties summarize what was just said, it increases the success of that communication tremendously; this applies to meetings, e-mails, memos, and face-to-face discussions.

___We do not do any follow-up because it feels like confrontation.

___We do not follow up afterwards because we do not want to look incompetent or appear too negative.

**Solution:** Follow-up is simply checking back with people to ensure they understood and are using what was communicated.

___Communication can easily go wrong from two sources—barriers and you.

**Solution:** You and the other party are each 75 percent responsible for each communication.

___In a dysfunctional group or company, employees

___Hoard information as power.

___Withhold communication as a weapon.

___Purposely refuse to communicate to make one another look bad.

**Solution:** In an excellent company everyone feels informed and treats good communication as a part of their personal responsibility.

## Skill #3: Priority Management

**Nearly every professional has more to do and less time to do it. In addition, it seems like everything is due now!**

| Self-Assessment #3: How Do You Manage Your Time? | | |
|---|---|---|
| According to your personal view, rate which side of the spectrum your work style is like. | | |
| **I...** | **Rating Scale** | **I...** |
| Do one thing at a time | ├──────────┼──────────┤ | Do many things at a time |
| Concentrate on one job or one task | ├──────────┼──────────┤ | Am highly distractible and subject to interruptions |
| Take commitments seriously (deadlines, schedules) | ├──────────┼──────────┤ | Consider time commitments an objective to be achieved, if that is possible |
| Need lots of background information | ├──────────┼──────────┤ | Already have the information |
| Am committed to the job | ├──────────┼──────────┤ | Am committed to people and human relationships |
| Adhere religiously to plans | ├──────────┼──────────┤ | Change plans easily and often |
| Am concerned about disturbing others; follow rules about privacy and consideration | ├──────────┼──────────┤ | Am more concerned with those who I am close to (family, close friends) than with my personal privacy |
| Show great respect for private property; seldom borrow or lend | ├──────────┼──────────┤ | Borrow and lend things often and easily |
| Emphasize promptness | ├──────────┼──────────┤ | Base promptness on the relationship |
| Am accustomed to short-term relationships | ├──────────┼──────────┤ | Have strong tendencies to build lifetime relationships |

**Answer Key**

Visually notice where you rated yourself.

**Left Side**

If most of your ratings were on the left side of the Rating Scale you prefer working in a structured manner. The tasks you tackle are deadline oriented, time sensitive, and have a discreet endpoint. You dislike projects and tasks that lack deadlines and milestones.

**Your Challenge**

Managing your priorities means understanding that not every task requires time sensitivity. Many involve dealing with preserving or maintaining relationships and with quality instead of quantity.

> **Right Side**
>
> If most of your ratings were on the right side of the Rating Scale you prefer working in a less structured manner and the work you undertake is less time sensitive. You focus more on quality than quantity. Since relationships are more important than time, the results you create are on the softer side of accounting.
>
> **Your Challenge**
>
> Managing your priorities means you must differentiate every task into those that are time sensitive and those that are not. At times you will need to spend more energy and focus on deadlines and quantity, while worrying less about quality and relationships.

## *Urgent Does Not Mean Important*

In business, the one consistent thing that separates the effective professional from the ineffective one is the ability to execute their plans. This skill is important to the Controller. You want to be known as one who can be counted on to deliver what you promise. By applying this best practice, you will enhance your integrity, because people will know that when you start something, you will finish it, and that when you make a promise, you will fulfill it.

PRIORITY MANAGEMENT PRINCIPLES 1 AND 2 (AKA THE 66⅔ RULES)

- About ⅔ of the work you do each day (personal and business) is not a priority.

- Less than ⅓ of the work you do adds value to someone else.

Ouch!

THE FACTS OF LIFE ABOUT TIME

Considerable amounts of time are wasted by employees each day because their work is done in a vacuum. This means they lack a clear deadline and unstated criteria for success. Professionals who are excellent at executing their goals consistently have realistic deadlines that they use to measure, to gain focus, and to ensure they bring tasks to completion.

Professionals who get the job done with quality always have in mind specific criteria for success, so they know when the job is done.

Whatever you naturally become fixated on, you are naturally attracted toward. Therefore, when you focus your energy on obstacles, you spend precious time and energy on dealing with those obstacles. What you focus on is what you attract.

When you are clearly focused on the true objective, you do whatever is needed to get there with minimal wasted energy.

To maximize personal productivity, realize that 80 percent of your time is spent on the trivial. Analyze and identify which activities produce the most value to your company and then shift your focus so that you concentrate on the vital few (20 percent). Either delegate or discontinue doing the trivial many. You also spend more than 20 percent of your time on time wasters, especially when you are stressed about something. See how many of these time wasters plague you.

## TOP TIME WASTERS THAT HIDE WHAT IS IMPORTANT

A Hired Gun avoids these situations because each leads to ineffective use of their time.

- Clutter

- Disorganization

- Poor processes

- Badly designed systems

- Complexity

- Perfectionism

- Bad habits

- Lack of structure

- Lack of a plan

- Lack of planning

- Overzealousness

- Poor memory and not writing stuff down so you can locate it later

- Incompatibility between the time zone and the task

- Lack of communication

- Lack of balance

- Lack of coordination

- Uncontrolled disruptions

- Continual stops and starts

### *Finance's Workload Killers that Create False Urgency*

Another pitfall that Controllers need to be aware of is those areas that utilize a tremendous amount of your team's time and energy. By proactively planning for and addressing the following productivity-sapping events, you will be able to keep your team and yourself on track:

- Mergers and acquisition activity

- Year-end closing

- Inventory taking and costing

- Peak sales season activity and transactions

- Sales promotion initiatives

- Budget development (this is becoming a year-round activity)

- Annual planning process (this, too, is becoming a year-round activity)

- Employee education, including job cross-training

- Externally imposed deadlines for compliance purposes

    - For example, SEC reports, IRS filings, shareholder's reports and analyses, management reports

- Personal time off.

    - For example, vacations, holidays, weather closings (This you cannot anticipate, but can plan for.)

- Meetings infinitum

    - For example, managers, executive, team, board, committee, task force, all-hands

## Skill #4: Leadership

**"Leaders are born not created. Everyone is a potential leader."**
**Ron Rael, Leadership Coach**

Anyone can become an effective, forceful leader with work and effort. Leadership is much broader than being a manager.

A leader is a person with vision, who gets people inspired and committed to that vision and then moves people from point A to point Z in a way where everyone benefits and grows from the experience.

Since this is not a book on leadership, we will concentrate on a few key leadership abilities that will be required of the part-time or contract Controller.

### *Traits of the Effective Finance Leader*

To be seen as a leader, you must

- Have a clear vision of what you want.

- Be fully accountable for your own results.

- Understand and use systems.

- Be an excellent communicator.

- Create opportunities for others.

> **Answer These Questions**
>
> How do these leadership traits relate to the responsibilities of the part-time Controller?
>
> How do these leadership traits relate to the responsibilities of the contract Controller?

## 1. HAVE A CLEAR VISION OF WHAT YOU WANT

One trait that the great leaders clearly have is the ability to create a vision. Tied to this is the ability to then articulate the vision clearly to others. As a Hired Gun you have put yourself in a difficult situation where you must clearly provide value to each client for every hour you invest in them. With each engagement, you will not fully know what to expect until you have been there for a while.

As you research the problems and begin to understand the situation, you must always start out with a clear vision of what you hope to do for them. Of course this may change as soon as you understand the conditions and limitations, but you still need to have an image of what you are going to do for them in terms of specific deliverables.

Even when you are just filling a chair for someone who is on leave or while the company is searching for a replacement, your vision is to keep the work flowing and ensuring that nothing slips through the cracks.

A very important piece of this specific leadership skill is to articulate your vision. At the beginning of the engagement, write out what you plan to do for your client. Of course, if you have developed an engagement letter or Scope of Work, this, in effect, is your vision. On a regular basis, be sure to look at that document to remind you of what you are doing and going to accomplish.

In those situations where you are working as part of a team, you must be able to describe what you intend to accomplish. You cannot just do this in writing. You represent a change that is threatening to most employees. They will be fearful of what you may ask them to do, and they will filter your memos or e-mails. As a leader, it is very important that you tell your visions and plans to people. In this moment of truth, each member of your team will decide whether or not they can trust you and whether or not you believe that you can accomplish what you describe.

This face-to-face articulation of your vision is an important milestone in every engagement you accept.

## 2. BE FULLY ACCOUNTABLE FOR YOUR OWN RESULTS

> **"Empowerment is a belief that our survival is in our hands, not someone else's, that we have a purpose that is compelling, and that we are committed to our purpose."**
>
> *The Empowered Manager*, Peter Block

*What Accountability Is and Is Not*

In true accountability, excuses and blame do not exist.

There is a tremendous amount of misunderstanding as to what accountability is. People frequently and mistakenly believe that accountability is about the other person. Accountability is about you. Sadly, in today's world we have very little support for the value of accountability. If you look at the popular media you will see example after example of a person who is not accountable and being rewarded for behaving that way. This sends a message to others that it is okay to act as the victim or to neglect personal responsibility. The blame game runs rampant throughout society. We tend to blame others for our misfortunes or for the ups and downs of life. For example, many people lost money during the dotcom bust. However, currently some lawyers, who specialize in class action lawsuits, are attempting to place blame on whoever has deep pockets. They are recruiting potential litigants on television in order to support these allegations through a class action suit.

"It takes a village to raise a child." This proverb applies especially to accountability. It takes a whole group of people to help hold someone accountable. This applies at every level: family, team, company, community, and society. At its very essence, accountability means accounting for my actions. Whenever you say that you want someone to be accountable, in effect, you are saying, "I expect you to account to me for the action you took or the decision you made." In society we make it easy for ourselves and others to not account for our decisions or actions for a variety of reasons. Recently, bad behavior has been given a new name: *intermittent explosive disorder*. This means people who cannot control their temper can use a physical limitation or disability as a way of accounting for their bad behavior. They can turn to a doctor and ask for a drug that will control their behavior which they claim they cannot control.

This section is not about changing society, but about leading your team and how you build accountability as a trait and expectation.

Let us start out with some important definitions to help you understand exactly what accountability is and how it fits into the scheme of someone's effectiveness.

**Accountability defined.** Accountability is keeping my word, meeting *our* commitments, and taking full ownership for my actions. Accountability is accepting reality (what is) without finding fault, placing blame, or hiding from the truth.

The first part of this definition is something that you could have written yourself. Every professional understands, at an intuitive level, that we must follow through on our commitments. Notice however that the first part of the definition says: meeting *our* commitments. What this means is that once the company has taken a stand on something, or the team has chosen a policy, you must support it 110 percent, even if you disagree with the policy or stand. This is required because you are an integral part of the company and team. So if you disagree with a policy and demonstrate to others your lack of support, you damage the integrity of the entire company. Therefore, you must instill in everyone that once a decision is made, no matter how unpopular, everyone is accountable for supporting it.

The second part of the definition is something most people cannot articulate when asked to define accountability. This is because in business, as well as society, we are so used to playing the blame game: whenever things go wrong we automatically find a scapegoat. Governments, individuals, leaders, managers, supervisors, and employees in business play this game. This part of accountability's definition says Murphy's Law exists and things will go wrong. When bad things happen, as they will, the accountable person will focus on solving the problem first and foremost. Yes, we do want to hold the person accountable who made a bad choice or error in judgment. However, the quicker your team stops playing the blame game and gets into the solution mode, the more effective your team will be.

Another way to understand the definition of a nebulous term like accountability is to examine its polar opposite. The exact opposite of being accountable is being a victim. The victim is the person who takes absolutely no ownership for what they do, what they say, or how they behave.

Do you want a person who behaves like that on your team?

**Responsibility defined.** People who choose to be less than accountable often claim to be accountable. However their actions show differently. Responsibility is living up to one's duty and following the rules. *Responsibility is doing the minimum.*

We all want employees on our team who are responsible. Yet I am sure that you have worked with people who tell you, "I will not do that task because it is *not* my job!" This employee is doing the bare minimum, as defined by their job description. Yet by the definition of the word, they are being responsible or living up to the duty. To have an effective team everyone must be willing to go beyond the bare minimum to get the job done. Therefore, accountability is a much higher and harder standard for people to reach because it goes well beyond personal responsibility.

### *Why Accountability Works to Make Everyone Successful*

While it may seem obvious that accountability helps to build a successful team and company, let us review a few of the most important benefits. Accountability

- Establishes individual integrity.

- Contributes to corporate integrity.

- Ensures employees follow through on their commitments.

- Guarantees people can rely on the team.

- Allows the team leader to spend less time acting as their supervisor.

- Builds employees who are dependable, yet can act independently.

- Reminds employees to hold themselves and each other accountable.

*10½ Realities of Accountability*

1.  We currently live in a riskless society where people feel someone else should pay for their losses. Issues of accountability are all around us. The starting point is awareness.

2.  Without a common, understood, and accepted definition of accountability, you will never be able to effect any change to it.

3.  Accountability is a nebulous concept until we define what it means for us. It is like quality—"I know it when I see it." A common definition gives us a basis for understanding and communicating.

4.  In order to impact accountability in others, I have to take an honest look at myself first and understand how others see me and my actions.

5.  Before I can do anything about our accountability, I must open my eyes to the level of accountability my team demonstrates in our daily actions and decisions.

6.  Improving accountability in others begins when I choose to be accountable each day.

7.  Once I decide to question another person's accountability, I automatically give them permission to question my accountability and account for my behaviors. Addressing accountability in someone else is like opening Pandora's Box; you may not like what you find inside (of yourself).

8.  When we find fault with each other, we decrease accountability. Focusing on the problem or issue without placing blame will help us to create solutions quicker.

9.  As long as we continue to focus on what is not working and place blame for things that go wrong, we cannot move forward in enhancing accountability.

10. We become immersed in our culture and soon lose sight of what it is like. It is critical to step back and regularly reexamine the culture ideals to see if they are building or hurting accountable behaviors and decisions.

    10½.Strengthening accountability starts with me.

*How Leaders Improve Accountability*

Since accountability is something that is impacted by what I do and say, it is very important for me, the leader, to take the first step and model what accountable behavior looks like. Below are a few specific suggestions of things that you, as a team leader and executive, can do to show that you take accountability seriously. By modeling these behaviors, you communicate the expectation that grants you the permission to hold others accountable.

The primary thematic ways to impact accountability are

**Monitor your own actions.** As a leader, you must be very self-aware of the way you act and words you speak. Leaders are highly visible and employees take their cue about acceptable behaviors from the leader. For example, if you refuse to engage in the blame game and go immediately to resolution, you show others that this is the accepted norm. For example, if you support every policy, even the ones that impact you negatively, you model that everyone needs to support the firm's policies.

- Meet all your own commitments.

- Be consistent in your words and actions.

- Catch people doing things right.

- Identify and remove barriers to honesty.

- Be open to new ideas.

**Use honesty**. You must always tell the truth. Of course, there are things that employees do not need to know or that may be withheld for legal or strategic purposes. Even in these exceptions, you must always strive to tell the employees the truth. This does not give you permission, however, to be blunt and rude. Leaders also use tact in being honest. By being honest and expecting honesty back from others, you set the expectation that you value the truth. The one thing nearly everyone despises is a negative surprise. Honesty helps to decrease the likelihood of this occurring.

- Instill and value honesty in others.

- Accept differing opinions and views.

- Seek solutions instead of blame.

- Give timely and honest feedback.

**Hold people's feet to the fire.** As a team leader, you wish to gain the respect of each member of the team. This does not mean that you let them walk all over you or take advantage of you. Holding people accountable means that you apply tough love. There are times when you must hold an employee's feet to the fire.

For example, if you request the XTZ report from Stuart by Friday, do not allow him to come to you Friday morning and say, "Is it okay if I get the XTZ report to you Monday afternoon? I have been super busy and haven't gotten to it yet." The team leader who wants to be popular will say, "Stuart, that is okay. I know you have been busy." By doing this, you undermine the accountability of your team because you did not enforce your expectation of timeliness and real-time communication, especially if this is the first time you were aware that Stuart is unable to meet the deadline he committed to.

Create a culture where accountability is the accepted norm and any employee who does not practice that norm is easily identified, so that they can be quickly unhired!

- Give employees authority with responsibility.

- Require employees to meet their commitments.

- Do not accept excuses or less than full efforts.

- Set measurable targets with and for each employee.

- Let employees know exactly what you expect from them.

- Do not use excuses for your errors and mistakes—own up to them.

## 3. UNDERSTAND AND USE SYSTEMS

Accounting is more than a profession. The accounting function is a set of systems that, if working optimally, produces some amazing results. An accounting department where the systems are not working well or are ineffective produces sad results.

If you have survived and thrived in accounting, then you understand systems. Being successful as a Hired Gun requires you to increase your awareness of the importance that systems play in accounting. Everything you touch in the accounting function is either an input or output of a system.

A great way to add value to your client is to go in with a fresh perspective and thoughtfully examine the quality of their systems. Then give them concrete suggestions for improvement. It is even better if you are asked to implement those improvements.

Most systems within the accounting function are either marginally effective or need major improvements. The quicker that you can implement these improvements or suggest them, the more the client will appreciate your efforts.

The three specific systems that the Controller relies on most are covered earlier in this chapter.

## 4. BE AN EXCELLENT COMMUNICATOR

**Your competence shows through how you communicate. What does yours say about you?**

Today's workplace depends dearly on competent communication! Yet listening is the most neglected communication skill. For example,

- 40 percent of jobs today require excellent listening skills.

- 30 percent of jobs today require excellent applied technology skills.

**Source:** John Stevens and AICPA

To be successful as the Hired Gun, you must communicate well and often. Yet, most people lack the understanding of how to improve their ability to be heard and understood. Please refer to Self-Assessment #4.

### Are You a Competent Communicator?

Effective communication can only begin after all the issues—major and minor ones—are on the table to be covered honestly. Refuse to make any commitments until you feel that you have received a complete list of all the points or issues that need to be addressed. A competent communicator knows how to say to the other party: "I would feel the same way if I were in your shoes."

The hallmarks of a professional committed to competent communication are the first seven traits in the self-assessment.

| Self-Assessment #4: How Well Do You Really Communicate? | | | | |
| --- | --- | --- | --- | --- |
| Complete this assessment by looking at how you communicate through the eyes of your employees and friends. Just imagine how a close friend or co-worker would describe your communication skills—both verbal and written—under normal everyday conditions. | | | | |
| **You practice** | **Always** | **Often** | **Occasionally** | **Rarely** |
| Proactive communication | | | | |
| Focuses the discussion on the customer | | | | |
| Understanding reality over perception | | | | |
| Facing each issue head-on | | | | |
| Relying on and using feedback to improve | | | | |
| Assertive communication | | | | |
| Open communication | | | | |
| Genuineness (even when not communicating) | | | | |
| Sincerity | | | | |
| Narrowing in on substance (the essence of what you talk about) | | | | |
| Using attracting behaviors (vs. distracting ones) | | | | |

**Answer Key:**

If you honestly rated yourself, as others see you, in the "Occasionally" or "Rarely" columns, then you are not an effective communicator. If you feel that you need to change any of these, start improving today!

The steps to changing how you communicate are shown at the end of this section.

To be trusted in your communication, you need to look at your overall package of how you are seen by others. This includes these important and hard to self-diagnose traits, which are the last four traits in the self-assessment.

**Communication Principle 1.** Humans typically tolerate many diverse behaviors, but the one not tolerated is when a person is being fake or not genuine, followed closely by lack of sincerity.

*Indicators of Your Communication-Related Behaviors*

Review these indicators and compare them with how you normally communicate in the work setting. If you really want to know for sure, give this list to a friend or colleague and have them check the indicators for you.

**The Assertive Communicator (Good Application of Skill)**

- Is direct and honest.

- Clearly communicates respect for all beliefs.

- Gives visual responses and cues when communicating.

**The Non-Assertive Communicator (Poor Application of Skill)**

- Is passive in communicating.

- Gives little visual responses and cues when communicating.

- Fails to reveal true thoughts and feelings.

**The Aggressive Communicator (Poor Application of Skill)**

- Uses overt and hostile communication in words and cues.

- Criticizes, humiliates, or dominates the listener.

- Violates the rights of others.

> **Answer This Question**
> Which type of communicator are you? How do you know this?

*Crucial Commutation Skill—Listening*

**Keys to Active Listening.** When a person is actively listening, 100 percent of their being is involved. Hearing is a physiological reaction, while listening is a mental process.

- Do not let yourself be distracted.

- Focus on the ideas (concepts) and not the person.

- Apply full attention to the speaker.

- Have the desire to listen.

- Take notes if you need to.

- Probe for details.

- Use your body to engage in the process of questioning.

*Process for Improving or Changing Your Communication Patterns*

The process for improving or changing your communication patterns involves

- Becoming aware of your communication patterns.

- Understanding that your style has both an upside and downside in business and work and how it impacts others.

- Asking a trusted friend for honest feedback on your style and listen without judgment.

- Selecting a new specific communication behavior.

- Practicing that new behavior continuously for 21 days.

## 5. CREATE OPPORTUNITIES FOR OTHERS

| | |
|---|---|
| **Self-Assessment #5: Can You Delegate?** | |
| Check off any and all reasons that you have not successfully handed off tasks, responsibilities, assignments, or projects to those who work for or under you. | |
| | I do not have time to delegate. |
| | They are too busy with their own work. |
| | Explaining it takes longer that doing it. |
| | It needs to be done right. |
| | No one else can be trusted with this. |
| | No one else can do it like I can. |
| | I cannot find someone with the proper skills. |
| | I cannot find someone with the right attitude. |

**Answer Key**

If you have used any of the excuses, or reasons, then you are not a good delegator. Failing to hand off work to others means two things:

1. You will always be behind and rarely make money as a Hired Gun, and
2. You will not be able to create opportunities for others to grow their skills and abilities.

You will discover what is really going on with you at the end of this section.

*You Cannot Do It All*

As a contractor who is asked to take on supervisory responsibilities for employees, it is easy to get yourself mired in many of the day-to-day minutiae. As you well know, delegating to the client's employees will help you stay above it all.

There is a way to see this differently, which will in turn make you more effective. Instead of delegating work, see your responsibility as creating opportunities for others. Instead of handing work to someone, recognize this as a chance for them to grow their skills. The difference is in your attitude.

We will start out by understanding the difference between delegating and creating opportunities so you can see why this distinction will benefit you as a Hired Gun.

### What Delegation Is and Is Not

*Did the ancient Egyptians, who built the pyramids, create opportunities for the people who actually did the work?*

No, they *assigned* work to them!

*Do you delegate work or do you create opportunities for your employees to grow, further their talents, and grow their skills?*

In today's business world, you need to do more than just delegate. *(As a leader, you must act as if your employees are volunteers.)* The way to get your team members to take on more responsibility and greater challenges is to create growth opportunities for each employee, which is much more beneficial than delegating.

The phrase "to delegate" derives from the Latin term "to appoint a deputy" and from English term "to give a bequest." Since you are not in the habit of giving a bequest or appointing a deputy for a particular task, *why are you* delegating work? If you are simply trying to get a task off your desk and find a body to do the work, then you are truly delegating.

Your goal as a supervisor is to instill in your employees the desire to take on more responsibility. The reason you choose this goal is so you can use your time more effectively and do more strategic types of work. Considering that the typical Controller and their team spend between 60 percent and 77 percent of their time on mundane, routine, and non-value-added tasks, it makes sense for you to reduce the time wasted and go to more value-adding tasks.

### Does the Task Add Value?

Let us quickly review a few key terms that are the basis for you to create opportunities for others. Start by looking at the activity or task. You want to ensure, as a supervisor, that every task you give to another person is one that adds value to someone else.

Value-added activities are those that are absolutely essential to the creation of your product. The product is the end state or deliverable that your internal customer wants, such as a report, a paycheck, a vendor check, an invoice, or a balanced general ledger. However, not every task that someone on our team performs benefits a customer. There are many tasks we perform each day that are considered non-value added activities—those actions that are not absolutely essential to the creation of our product.

Even in an Action Plan, which identifies the steps to complete the plan, you must instill in your team the desire to only tackle steps that add value. Value-added steps are those that usually change the product in some way toward what your customer wants. Because accountants tend to be detail oriented, we think we need to cross every T and dot every I. The real question that you must instill in each team member is to continually ask, "Does my crossing of this T or dotting of this I change or improve the product so that we meet the customers' expectation?"

### The Difference Is in Your Attitude

Whenever you give an employee a work assignment you create a master-servant relationship. The act of delegation creates a master-agent relationship. I would expect that you are not trying to create a master-servant relationship with each of your employees. Instead, you want them to become more dependable and professional. The attitude that you, their supervisor, must adopt is that they are your peers. To an employee, delegation feels like you are handing them a task that is beneath you and then abandoning them. Creating an opportunity feels to your employee like you are inviting them to go on a trip with you.

Try this with someone: Hand the person a piece of paper and tell them out loud, "I delegate this to you." Then, with that same person, hand them a piece of paper and tell them out loud, "I have an opportunity for you." Ask the individual how the two approaches feel and what the difference between the two approaches is. The answer, I guarantee, is that they appreciate the second approach over the first. (Obviously, your wording would be more tailored to the situation.)

You will discover that you will be a more effective team leader by adopting the attitude that, instead of making someone else do your work via delegation, you are creating an opportunity for the employee to grow their skills and expand their knowledge. Think back to those early days of your career and recall your intense curiosity about how things worked and how much you wanted to tackle new challenges so you could prove your worth to those you worked for. The reason you became the competent Controller or CFO you are today is due to the opportunities that these farsighted individuals created for you. This is the attitude you must maintain to build dependable and competent members of your team.

### *Why Creating Opportunities Works to Build a More Effective Finance Team*

One reason accounting work is so stressful is because we look at our job in a limiting way. As the leader of your team, you must continually remind them of this fact: "Your work is really about making a difference in people's lives." When employees finally get and internalize the message that they make a difference in someone's life, they will understand that the work they do adds value. By looking for ways that your team members can contribute more, take on more responsibilities, and expand their knowledge, you will help to reinforce this attitude about making a difference. In addition, you will help to reduce the level of stress that many accounting team members feel about the work they do. Creating opportunities for others works to help team members (including you) see their job much more expansively by focusing on the benefits they provide to others.

Even if you do not buy into the argument about creating opportunities for others over delegating, you still want to ensure that you delegate in ways that will foster an attitude of service in every team member. You can accomplish this by looking at the top reasons why supervisors fail to delegate and instead try to do everything themselves. Use this as a self-test to see how many of these excuses you have used when you decided not to delegate or create an opportunity for someone.

### *Reasons Why a Leader Fails to Delegate or Create Opportunities*

If you checked any of the excuses in Self-assessment #5, here is what you are doing and why.

**Reason 1: You Lack Experience.** You lack seasoning, do not know any better, or are uncomfortable delegating.

**Reason 2: You Have Insecurities.** You fear failure, are timid, are unsure, or are working at a level beyond your capabilities and skills.

**Reason 3: You Suffer from Workaholism.** For you, work is all-consuming, you are a perfectionist, or are too serious and have no time for silliness or frivolity.

**Reason 4: You Suffer from Vanity.** You desire all the credit or glory, consider yourself to be self-important, or are arrogant.

**Reason 5: You Display Artificiality.** You deliberately use camouflage, develop fall guys, or assign unreasonable deadlines.

**Warning:**

Each of these excuses are a career-limiting attribute! These traps will limit your success as Hired Gun.

## 7½ Priority Management Myths

| **Myth #1** | **To be effective you must keep a To-Do list.** |
|---|---|
| **Reality** | **A Priority List is what you need to keep and focus on!** |

It is your priorities that drive what you need to be doing.

> **Example:** You say that your health is a priority but your To-Do list is long and you never get time to exercise. Are your to-dos interfering with your priorities? No! You have simply not made health a priority. Instead, if you look at your Priority List each morning and see health on it, you will find the time in your schedule each day to do something healthy.

| **Myth #2** | **Multitasking helps you get more done.** |
|---|---|
| **Reality** | **Multitasking is unproductive and harms your brain!** |

Several recent studies have found this to be true and the problem is growing. Doing a task properly and completely requires concentration. When you multitask, you cannot fully concentrate because you are trying to think of several things at once. People who multitask suffer from confusion as well as the inability to relax and to concentrate. Try this. Plan out your day leaving enough time to concentrate on your priorities; you will get things done faster. Keep a list of little things that also need to get done, because you have small spaces of time in your schedule to fit those small things in. Better yet take a breather in those spare moments to clear your thoughts for the next big task.

| **Myth #3** | **Unless there are other people involved, you do not need to prepare a time budget for your own projects and major activities.** |
|---|---|
| **Reality** | **Big projects and intensive tasks consume as much time as you have available!** |

Unless you proactively limit your time of involvement because big projects and major tasks consume as much time as you give them. Instead of letting that happen, prepare a time budget and just before that time limit has been met, wrap things up. You will find that by knowing in advance you only have ten hours to spend on a project, magically you will only spend ten hours.

**Myth #4        Doing time wasting activities is natural and to be expected.**

**Reality        Wasting time means that you are scared!**

When you procrastinate over something important and find yourself wasting time, you are afraid of that important thing. There is something in that task that is impacting you—your self-image or your self-limitations. Instead of procrastinating, take time to look at what you are afraid of. Very often, your fear is irrational and by thinking about what terrifies you, you will become rational again.

**Myth #5        You are busier today because life is more complicated.**

**Reality        You, like everyone else, suffer from cognitive overload.**

The technology we use to be more productive also requires that we shift gears up about 100 times a day and face constant interruptions every few minutes. Instead of letting technology run your time, set aside times in each day where you will be totally uninterrupted. Turn off your iPod, e-mail, your phone, your PDA, and any other device that could interfere with your concentration.

**Myth #6        Managing your time is about allocating the hours available to the tasks you must complete.**

**Reality        True time management is about balance!**

Because of the demands on your time it is very easy to get out of balance. You may be spending every waking hour working or thinking about work and forget about your personal and family life. Instead, set a limit on how much time you devote to work each day and then use the rest of the day in personal pursuits. You will find that you have much more energy and mental bandwidth to deal with work issues.

**Myth #7        Managing your time carefully means that you should be able to accomplish everything on your to-do list that others deem important.**

**Reality        You have the same number of hours each day whether you do nothing or you do everything!**

You must decide how you want to spend your day. Instead of allowing others to dictate what you need to do, evaluate your business and personal priorities and make sure these coincide with what you are currently working on. If there is a discrepancy, ask yourself before each task: "What is the purpose of this? What am I really I trying to accomplish through this task? How does this help me in my current priority?"

**Myth #7½        If you feel pressed for time and too busy, it is just a condition of life.**

**Reality        How you spend your time is your choice!**

No one holds a gun to your head during the day. The choices you make each day are entirely up to you. Pause often to ask yourself: "What choices am I making and why am I making them?"

## Conclusion

The contract Controller's job is much more than just being a technician. There is a lot of self-management that needs to occur. Unlike running the department in a normal employee status or being a member of a CPA firm, you lack a team of support people working behind the scenes. Your success depends entirely on you.

The four skills that aid you in client engagements covered in this chapter: 1) focus, 2) systems building, 3) priority management, and 4) leadership are your support system. No matter how competent you are with the skills today, there are always things to learn and ways to improve. Take these skills to heart if you decide that being a contract financial executive is your cup of tea.

Even if you decide being a contractor is not what you choose to do, these four skills will serve you well in whatever career choices you make.

The next chapter will cover additional skills that will build upon this skill set.

# Chapter 7
# Hired Gun Skills—Part 2

**"I found out there is more to me than I imagined."**

**Ron Rael, Leadership Coach**

## Introduction

After completing this chapter you should be able to

- Apply the Gap Analysis to uncover your client's goals and deficiencies.

- Use a defined process to sell someone on your ideas and suggestions.

- Proactively manage the client's expectations.

- Find multiple ways to market yourself through social media, visibility, and networking.

## Dual Service Skill Cluster

In this chapter, we will concentrate on four high-level skills that may be new to the person wanting to become a contract Controller or CFO. **Yet, you will need these to be successful.** Whether you decide to continue as a Hired Gun, this skill set will serve you well throughout your career.

Several of these skills—selling your ideas, marketing, and managing client expectations—are usually foreign to the typical Controller. A comment I receive when covering these speaks volumes about how accountants typically define themselves.

*"If I wanted to sell something, I would have gone into marketing!"*

Mastering these high-level skills takes time and practice.

## More Special Skills the Hired Gun Needs

More special skills need by the Hired Gun include

- Future visioning

- Selling your solutions (convincing others about your ideas)

- Managing a client's expectations

- Marketing professional services

## Skill #5: Future Visioning

Many of the projects that you are hired for will be messes created by people who are visionary but lack the skills to bring their vision to fruition. American and European businesses would not exist without visionaries. American and European businesses would also not exist without people who can take a vision and convert this nebulous concept into tangible business plans and executable goals. The reason that you are a professional accountant is based on the fact that you have the skill to convert a vision into something tangible.

The following tool and best practice, titled the Gap Analysis, will enable you to convert someone's vision into reality by finding the elements that will be necessary to go from where the client is today to where they want to be in 18 to 36 months. Once you have mastered using the Gap Analysis you will find that you can quickly create a specific Action Plan to get someone where they want to go.

### *Hired Gun Tool: The Gap Analysis*

A Gap Analysis is a visual examination of the client's current state compared to their desired state. A Gap Analysis starts with the honest assessment of where the client is today. A Gap Analysis captures a clear vision of the future. The outcome of your Gap Analysis is to show what is missing and required to reach this vision.

### STEPS FOR PREPARING A GAP ANALYSIS

Steps for preparing a Gap Analysis include

1. Ask the client to describe the problem, issue, or area that they want to make progress on.

2. Ask the client to describe the benefits or reasons that they need to solve this problem and why they need to create an Action Plan for getting there.

3. If the client's dream is broad, ask them to focus on a particular aspect or element of their desired state. If the goal is too broad, the Action Plan will be also.

4. Ask the client to define their deadline for achieving this desired end state. This is actually the point in time they expect to arrive at this destination. Stick with 18 to 36 months.

5. As the Facilitator, ask the client to describe their current state of affairs as it relates to this end state or dream. Make sure that there is a balance of both their assets or positives and the areas that they are deficient. Keep the focus of today's status or reality on those things that contribute or detract from their desired end state. Work to keep them honest and grounded.

6. Again as Facilitator, ask the client to describe what their destination will look like. Ask questions such as "What will you have? What will it look like? How will it feel?" and "How will you know you have arrived?" Make sure to carry forward any assets or positives that they currently have into this future state.

7. Work with the client to fill in the middle section, called the missing links. As detailed as possible, identify specific actions or steps that must take place so they can go from today

to tomorrow. If you completed your Gap Analysis correctly, these bridges will pop out clearly to both you and the client.

8. Use the information that you filled in as missing links to create a specific formalized Action Plan. Set a priority to each of the major action steps, asking this question often, "What needs to happen before you take this step?"

9. Review and update this Gap Analysis on a regular basis with your client. Use it to check their progress and to see if there were other items in the missing links that were overlooked.

---

### Activity 7-1: Perils of Pauline, Part 7

Since you are already serving as her coach, you will perform a Gap Analysis of Pauline's skills and talents, as they exist today. She provided you with the information in columns 1 and 3, and you will provide her with the missing links or bridges to cross the gap in front of her.

Pauline's Area Analyzed: Go from being a solo Contract Accountant to creating a firm that provides contract accounting services.

| Pauline Today | The "Missing Links" | Pauline in 18 months |
|---|---|---|
| Energetic | | Energetic |
| Does not execute well | | Executes consistently |
| Risk-taker | | Risk-taker |
| Limited leadership experiences | | Confident leader |
| Management experience with financial teams only | | Confident manager |
| Somewhat visionary | | Visionary |
| Loves challenges | | Accepts challenges well |
| Works well with peers and those she supervises | | Works well with people at all levels |
| Diplomatic | | Diplomatic |
| Adequate communicator | | Effective communicator |
| Inconsistently disciplined | | Disciplined |
| Lacks willingness to listen | | Active listener |
| Timid at marketing | | Confident at marketing |
| Great at customer service | | Great at selling services |
| Easily makes lasting relationships | | Makes relationships that turns into business |
| Comfortable at schmoozing | | Uses schmoozing to create work for her employees |

**About Your Friend Pauline**

Burned out from the challenges and lack of support as a full-time employee, Pauline informs you,

*(continued)*

*(continued)*

"I really love being a Hired Gun! But I believe that I can do better by creating a stable of qualified controllers and CFO's who would work for me. This way they can focus on what they do best and not sweat marketing or looking for projects. I can capitalize on what I do best; create lasting relationships."

"Can you help me create an action plan on what I need to do to make this happen?"

**Your Assignment**

1. What advice would you give Pauline before she decides to follow her dream?

2. What gaps do you see in her overall skill set?

3. How can Pauline overcome this gap—where, when, and how? Fill in the missing links section of the Gap Analysis started above.

4. What other skills covered in this book could Pauline improve to move closer to fulfilling her vision?

## *Power in the Gap Tool*

The Gap Analysis is a fantastic best practice that every Hired Gun, Consultant, Controller, and CFO needs in their toolkit. By getting into the habit of using it to set your own goals when you take on projects, you will quickly be able to grasp the items that are needed to get you from where you are today to where you want to be tomorrow. It is a very powerful and insightful tool, which will help you to execute on your goals and achieve your vision.

Then you are able to assist your clients to do the same.

## Skill #6: Selling Your Solutions

> **"Nothing is more dangerous than an idea if it is the only one you have."**
> **Emile Chartier**

You will spend a lot of time attempting to convince other people about the worth and validity of your ideas.

Remember your role is as an outsider who is brought in to solve a specific problem or cleanup a distasteful mess. As an outsider you will need to recruit the help and support of others that you do not supervise or work with on a daily basis. Therefore the skill of selling your ideas is of utmost importance to the contract Controller. As I have stated several times, even if you decide not to be a contractor this particular skill will be valuable in whatever endeavors you pursue. Except for people who sell for a living, such as sales personnel and CEOs, the average person does not understand that there is a defined process to selling ideas.

Before we get into the process, let us do a quick summary of the person who will engage you to work for their organization. Understanding this person's mindset will enable you to do a good job of selling your ideas to that person.

## *The Mindset of the Risk-Taking Entrepreneur*

Call it a genetic compulsion, a defensive reaction, or simple optimism, but the reality is that most business owners refuse to contemplate the possibility of failure. It is as if the word does not exist in their vocabulary. Failure is an option. The downside of this "never-say-die" attitude is that it can be ruinous, wasteful, costly, hurt people, and spoil opportunities for future success.

Most entrepreneurs see themselves as the type of person who put their heads down and charge full steam ahead. However you can badly injure yourself with that mindset. This person does not avoid risk, but ignores it at every opportunity. This person fails to recognize that failure is an option, and this is why risk can be mismanaged or unacknowledged.

In facing up to the possibility of failure in risk-taking, there is a very delicate line to walk. It is better to assume failure can occur than to resign yourself to it. It is okay to acknowledge our fear but not let ourselves be overcome by it. Walking that line requires courage.

### CONVINCING THIS MINDSET

Selling your ideas to a business owner or anyone who is a chronic risk-taker requires you to speak in terms of possibilities. These folks are visionaries and they do not like people to diminish their dreams. While you speak about the real world, the risk-taker does not care about reality. They focus on what can occur and close themselves off from what cannot occur. They want to focus on a vision, but they do not sweat the details of how to make the impossible possible. Therefore, the way to sell your ideas is to also speak their language of possibilities.

> **Example:** Your project is to make an accounting department more productive and reduce the time (from seven days to three) it takes for them to issue reports. You have done this before and now you must convince the CEO to support you and to understand the hard work that needs to occur to make this happen.

**Wrong way:** "Mr. Johnson, I know how to bring this accounting team up to a higher level of productivity. Within six weeks I will be able to reassign responsibilities, modernize the information flow, help people understand their jobs better, and get your reports out faster."

Before you finish saying this, Mr. Johnson's eyes have glazed over and his mind has moved on to the next thing. Your mistake was to speak about how you would do it.

**Right way:** "Mr. Johnson, within three months you will have reports on your desk that not only highlight what is working but also identify specific problem areas. These reports will be so easy to read that you can identify the major trends while drinking your first cup of coffee each morning."

Mr. Johnson will ask you some questions. "Are you sure you can do this? What is this gonna cost us in terms of time, money, and confusion?" Now you can have a meaningful dialogue with Mr. Johnson about the changes that need to be made.

In the first scenario, you did not speak Mr. Johnson's language of what is possible. In the second scenario, when you did paint a picture of the future to Mr. Johnson's liking, you had his full attention so that you could talk to him about what you need to make it happen.

*Their Pain*

When I mention their pain, this refers to the fact that your client's executives, managers, and employees have problems that are not getting resolved. As their problem solver, you are the logical choice and most qualified person they rely on to help them get rid of their pain. You understand how the business operates, you understand how the finances work, and you (hopefully) understand the key players (decision-makers and what makes them tick). One of the most rewarding aspects of the Hired Gun job is to be regarded as the resource that employees think of first when they need a solution which they are unable to find themselves.

## *Process for Selling Your Ideas*

As stated earlier there is a defined process for selling your ideas. The starting point is to identify the pain. Here is why:

**People and organizations will not change until the pain outgrows their tolerance.**

If you do not fully understand their pain, the client's tolerance level, or the cause of the pain you will not be successful in selling change to anyone. To be successful in selling your ideas, you must become masterful in quickly sizing up a situation to determine those three things. Once you have a handle on them, you will be able to sell anything to anyone who is in pain.

In figure 7-1 the process is shown graphically. The center of your diagram is your starting point. Then you go straight up and follow the diagram clockwise.

**Figure 7-1**

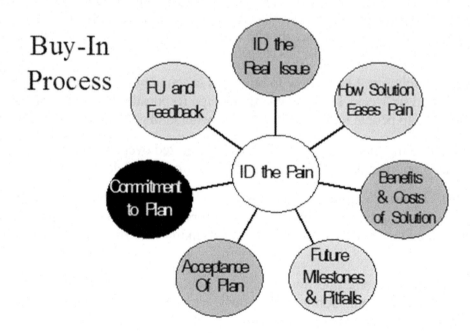

**Warning!** When speaking with your client, do not use the word pain. Use terms like possibilities and unexploited opportunities. The moment you say the word pain, you will scare people off. Everyone hates pain, or so they believe, yet the idea of making a change is more distasteful than putting up with the problem in the first place.

In the following steps, I use the phrase change plan to describe the work that you will be doing for them. This process works whenever you want to convince someone of any idea.

STEP 1: IDENTIFY THE PAIN

As a diagnostician, your first step is to get a quick understanding of what the client is worried about. To accomplish this you must have a list of specific probing questions that will help the client to explain to you what is really going on.

Sample questions you ask:

- *What keeps you awake at night about this issue?*

- *How long has this problem been going on?*

- *What attempts have been made to solve this particular problem in the past?*

- *Why does this problem continue to crop up?*

- *What has prevented you or the organization from doing something about this problem before now?*

- *What happens if this problem does not get solved quickly?*

STEP 2: IDENTIFY THE REAL ISSUE

The client will often only speak to you about the effects of the pain and not the cause of the pain. Like in our body when something starts hurting, we really notice it and pay strict attention to it. Over time, the pain seems to diminish and we only remember it at certain times. The problem that causes the pain is still there but we have numbed ourselves to its effect, at least temporarily.

Once the client has given you an understanding of what they think the problem is, it is incumbent on you to do some more investigation to find the root cause. With your wide experience and knowledge you should be able to identify initially what the source is or may be.

STEP 3: DETERMINE HOW YOUR SOLUTIONS SOLVE THE PROBLEM

Because you are a smart, talented person, you will quickly arrive at several solutions to the client's problems. In order to sell the client on your change plan, you must be able to answer to their full satisfaction how your solutions will both solve the problem now and prevent it in the future.

The only way to make this happen is to understand the source of their pain. If you do not understand the true source, the problem will likely occur again and as the consultant you will be blamed for this.

STEP 4: DETERMINE THE COSTS AND BENEFITS

**People only change when the benefits clearly outweigh the costs.**

Inherent in solving the problem are the benefits which the client wants and the costs which the client does not want. In your cost and benefit analysis, never fail to overlook the soft intangible and emotional costs. The emotional and intangible costs of changing are more likely to prevent a client from acting on your suggestions than the hard measurable costs.

Yet the intangible benefits of making the change will almost always outweigh and outnumber the tangible and measurable benefits.

As a rule of thumb, your list of benefits should exceed the costs by a ratio of 2 to 1. If you are unable to define more benefits than costs, then you are either not seeing the problem clearly or you do not have sufficient experience in solving this type of problem.

This 2 to 1 ratio is important since the client will diminish or minimize about a third of your benefits because they are looking at their problem from the inside-out, while you are looking at the issue from the outside-in. Their judgment is clouded by the pain and, more importantly, by their own contributions to the problem. Ego and hubris prevent the client from seeing all the possible benefits.

## STEP 5: DEFINE THE MILESTONES AND PITFALLS

If you fail to take steps 5, 6, and 7, you will end up with egg on your face and with the blame for the problem lingering or growing.

In step 5 you must honestly tell the client what to expect in the future. As an experienced change agent you know that every time you change one thing at least one or more other things change as well. Some of these unplanned changes are not for the better. In selling your ideas to your client, you must be able to identify the milestones along the way.

*What will things look like 30 days from now, 60 days from now, and one year from now?*

You also must honestly talk about the pitfalls that the client will expect and need to start addressing now. For example, if you take on the responsibility for reorganizing an accounting department, you know intuitively that employees will resist the change. Angry employees will actually undermine your work. You must be honest and tell the client that this will happen and is expected. If you fail to make this disclosure, then when it happens the client will think that you are the one who messed up or caused it.

## STEP 6: OBTAIN ACCEPTANCE FOR THE PLAN

In step 6, you must look for specific acceptance from the client for your ideas and suggestions. Being a seasoned veteran will benefit you here. The client may be nodding while saying, "Yes, I want you to proceed with this project." However, you notice his body language says otherwise. You notice that he cannot look you straight in the eye. You notice that when you bring up certain subjects he looks very uneasy.

What you are witnessing is that the client has not accepted your plan. All too often in business, around seven times out of ten, the person you are asking for something will agree to it just to get you out of their face. They have no intention of doing whatever you ask, but it is far easier in their mind to say "yes" knowing that they do not intend to do it then to say "no" directly to your face. Sad but true.

This is why you must spend time making sure that you do have 100 percent acceptance of your change plan.

STEP 7: OBTAIN COMMITMENT TO THE PLAN

Just because you have acceptance of the plan does not guarantee that you have the client's commitment. Acceptance is a mental process. Commitment is an emotional process. As a Hired Gun and their designated change agent, you must work to determine that the client has actually committed to your plan for change.

Your first commitment indicator is when the client gives you money. Money has such an emotional component to it that when we give someone money it usually means we are emotionally committed to whatever the money is given for.

Another key indicator of commitment is when the client takes the first few steps, which are often the hardest.

A third indicator of commitment is when you obtain the client's signature to the change plan. This is why using an engagement letter along with the scope of work will help you to be very successful as a contract professional.

Over time you will find some other key indicators of commitment.

STEP 8: DO FOLLOW-UP AND COLLECT FEEDBACK

This last step is very easy for you to overlook because you are busy doing what the client asks. However, in your change plan you must build in specific methods for collecting feedback on how the change plan is going. Then on a regular basis, you share with your client the results of feedback—good and bad—and talk about the status of the plan.

As a contract Controller you should meet with your client at least once a week with status reports. This meeting is where you present your updates on the change plan or plans that you are leading for them.

In each of these follow-up sessions, check for the client's continuing acceptance of the plan and commitment to it. Do not assume that just because you obtained acceptance and commitment once that the client will not change their mind. As a client discovers the amount of work and effort that it takes to change something, so may their decision to change.

*When You Speak, Clients Will Listen*

Always remember that you are selling your ideas to a person that never says die and failure is not in their vocabulary. Part of your overall strategy for selling your client on your ideas is to meld your suggestions into the client's ideas, so that the clients feel they created the solution.

## Skill #7: Managing Client Expectations

**What you expect is not always what you get. What you get is always what you expect.**

## *You, the Scapegoat?*

This skill is allied with the previous one of selling your ideas. All too often for the inexperienced consultant—as well as for the experienced one—an implementation or project fails and the consultant is blamed. The failure can be directly traced to the client's improper implementation or the client's failure to take action and not on the soundness of the consultant's advice. This blame event occurs because, as Hired Guns, we do a poor job of managing the client's expectations.

> **Example:** If your client, say the CEO of an emerging organization, really understood the accounting function, there would not be a problem for you to solve. Since they do not have this insider knowledge, the problem of a poorly organized accounting department was allowed to exist, grow, and create other problems in the organization.
>
> If people on this team understood what it takes to prepare a realistic cost analysis, they would not need you.

### POOR PROBLEM DEFINITION

What I am asking you to understand is that rarely does the client understand the full extent of the problem that they are asking you to solve. This lack of knowledge includes

- The extent of the problem.

- The byproducts of the problem.

- The full cost to remove or solve the problem.

- The time it takes to remove or solve the problem.

- The conditions that created the problem in the first place.

- The conditions that led to the problem being overlooked for such a long time.

- What people are feeling and thinking about the problem.

- Ways that employees have creatively found to get around the problem.

- Specifics of what it will take to prevent the problem from reoccurring.

### YOU, THE MAGICIAN?

For whatever reason, companies that engage a Hired Gun to solve a particular problem assume that you carry a magic wand. Somehow, they believe that with your experience and knowledge, a few incantations, and your mojo will save them from themselves.

## *Tactics to Manage Expectations*

Armed with this information, to be successful as a contract Controller or CFO you must understand that a primary responsibility for your own success is to manage these unreasonable expectations. Doing so requires you to employ the following tactics:

- Undersell and over-deliver.

- Clearly define the client's expectations up front and clarify them with the client often.

- Clearly define your expectations up front and clarify them often.

- Give the client regular status reports.

- Invest significant hours at the beginning of the project to understand the politics that will be involved in getting the problem fixed.

- Ask your client the tough questions.

- Communicate and listen, then listen and communicate.

- Be willing to be the scapegoat or bad guy if necessary.

- Never rest on your laurels because there is always something that you have never seen before.

- Use a sounding board of other Hired Guns.

- Trust your intuition and check your facts.

- Instill accountability in the people who are assisting you in making the change.

- As soon as conditions change that affect the cost or scope, meet with the client immediately.

- Give the client multiple options and, once chosen, stick to them.

- Use empathy and see the issue through the client's eyes.

- Be flexible *and* firm.

- Put services before fees.

- Be willing to terminate the relationship if the client plays games.

## *Bad Karma for a Hired Gun*

You never want to be in a position where you are blamed for your client's blunders. Yet, you will be if you fail to manage the client's expectations of you. This skill goes hand-in-hand with selling your ideas.

Practice this skill often.

## Skill #8: Marketing Professional Services

Every new client is the start of a new relationship—similar to dating.

## *Marketing Yourself as a Part-Time or Contract Controller*

As mentioned earlier, marketing yourself as a part-time or contract Controller can be a pain or a delight. Marketing may not come naturally to you. Marketing takes a tremendous amount of time, energy, and self-assurance to do it successfully. In addition, there is no centralized marketplace for the job, as there is for the full-time Controller (regular employee) position.

**Companies in transition are the usual customers for a contract Controller!**

**Visibility and networking are the keys to marketing!**

| |
|---|
| **Activity 7-2: Help Me Pauline, Part 8** |
| How could Pauline market herself? |

This chapter will give you a variety of ideas on where to turn, whom to target, and tools to use. In the end, it will be your own ingenuity, tenacity, courage, and self-promotional skills that determine the amount of work you will attract.

FIRST, ADOPT A MARKETING MINDSET

To be a successful marketer of your own services, you must change how you view yourself and view marketing. With rare exception, accountants are not comfortable wearing the sales hat. If you were comfortable in marketing and selling—which are two different functions—you would have chosen a different career path.

In addition, studies have shown that it is easier for a person to sell someone else's product or service rather than their own. We will not go into the reasons, but it has to do with our self-image.

Now that you understand this, the next part is easy. *You must commit to seeing yourself as an Accountant Who Markets.* Adopting this mindset relieves a lot of pressure that you may have about needing to market your services to people that you do not know. The statement: "I am an accountant who markets" reminds you that you are a financial professional first and foremost.

Over the years, many people have extolled this truism, which still rings true today.

**Everyone has something to sell, so we are always selling something.**

To understand this marketing mindset that you must maintain, we will take a quick review of the difference between marketing and selling. People who do not understand this difference lump the two concepts together, or they think that selling is *trying to convince someone to buy something that they do not need*. The image we accountants often carry in our head of the typical salesperson is someone selling us either Amway or used cars. Nothing about marketing can be further from the truth.

SECOND, MARKETING AND SELLING HAVE DIFFERENT AIMS

*Objectives of Marketing*

Objectives of marketing include

- To position your services in a way that potential users see the need for them

- To convince potential users why they need to buy from you

- To be easy to find and contact

*Objectives of Selling*

Objectives of selling include

- To determine if the buyer's (clients) needs match your services and if your products fulfill the buyer's specific needs

- To convince the buyer (client) that your services and products will add value in ways that exceeds their investment

- To deliver no less than what was promised

- To be easy to work with

Now that you understand the difference, most of your efforts in gaining new clients will be to meet the objectives of marketing, which include positioning, branding, and being accessible.

**The difference is in your attitude! You control your attitude, always!**

The rest of this section is designed to offer you many ideas on how to best market your services. All of them work. Your task is to select the one or ones that you feel comfortable with. If you start each day with dread because you must spend time selling yourself to strangers, you will not be successful as a Hired Gun. If you start each day looking forward to telling people about how you can help them, you will be successful.

## *Ways to Market Your Services*

**Sorry, there is no magic or secret to selling a product or service.**

There are, however, things that you can do consistently that will help you create a brand or reputation that will increase the likelihood that engagement and projects will come your way, without too much stress and strain. These include

- Create Visibility

- Networking

- Social Media

- Partnering or Joint Venturing

- Exploit a Niche

## 1. HOW TO CREATE VISIBILITY TO POTENTIAL CLIENTS

*Marketing Through Visibility*

To obtain new clients, you must stay visible to both past clients and potential ones. So, you must make the most of your opportunities because visibility takes time away from doing the work.

- *Contact a client between 12 and 18 times a year*—Keeping up with clients helps prevent them from looking elsewhere for new solutions to their financial or operational problems. People's lives and their businesses change quickly, and reminding clients (potential and actual) of your existence helps them remember you when they need help.

- *Use a variety of approaches in your touches, so that you reach the potential clients in different ways throughout the year*—Examples: send an article, e-mail a newsletter, send an invitation, send a gift, drop-off a checklist, e-mail a website link, call to say hello, contact them with a referral.

- *Send something of interest or value*—Expand beyond their business or industry. Consider sending information on the client or prospect's interest or desires. Create a specialty e-zine that covers their personal interests.

- *Stand out from the crowd*—Do creative and fun things in your market to grab attention. Do not let your materials look generic or like anyone else's. Keep them unique but not outrageous. Examples:

  - Golf tees taped to your business card

  - Whimsical postcards

  - A crossword puzzle with insider terminology

  - A cartoon with an on-target punch line

- *Take advantage of e-mail, but do not overdo it*—People get so much e-mail that they tend to ignore it, trash it, or never take time to read it. Limit your e-mailing. Instead, send written notes and make phone calls.

- *Consider doing a joint promotion with other professionals*—Very often your client has a multitude of needs. Align yourself with another service provider to offer an integrated solution.

*Companies to Target with Visibility*

Companies to target with visibility include

- Where recent layoffs occurred

- Newly relocated to your area

- Currently experiencing downsizing

- Recently obtained a new, significant contract

- In major transition—merger, consolidation, sale

- Start-up companies

- Firms in bankruptcy or liquidation

- Where transactions are still done manually

- Firms that use Quicken or QuickBooks

### *Places or People to Make Yourself Visible To*

Places or people to make yourself visible to include

- Lending officers

- CPA firms with larger clients

- Corporate and bankruptcy attorneys

- Venture capital firms

- Management firms

- Management consultants

- Accounting specialist temporary agencies

- CFO service firms

- Contract CEOs and CFOs

- Finance recruiters

- Startup advisors

- Executive recruiters

- Young entrepreneurs

### *Develop Tools for Market Visibility*

Tools to develop for market visibility include

- Create a resume that is more like an advertisement piece.

- Read the *Business Journal* and similar local publications.

- Establish a formal network with other contract Controllers.

- Develop a needs assessment survey and offer to conduct for free.

- Develop your marketing message or 10-second commercial.

- Get involved in an accounting or finance association.

- Volunteer where you can work with CEOs.

- Use your telephone to make networking calls daily.

- Have a website with full information and diagnostic tools.

- An ongoing online dialogue with potential clients.

*Create Visibility by Giving It Away*

Today, several successful business models believe that making money later is more important than making money today.

Things You Can Give Away Easily

Things you can give away easily include

- Book chapters

- Articles

- Partial checklists

- White papers

- Case studies

- Simple diagnostics tools

- Brown bag presentations

- Free hour of consultation

- Sample reports

## 2. HOW TO CREATE OPPORTUNITIES VIA NETWORKING

*Market by Taking Advantage of Networking Opportunities*

Develop and fine-tune your marketing message or 10-second commercial.

*What do you say if you have to deliver a message in 10 seconds or less?*

Today, with everybody on Internet time, we give each person from three to ten seconds to determine if they are worth our time.

Let us say you meet someone at a networking event, and you want them to notice you so you can see if they might need a contract Controller or your expertise.

*How do you do that besides offering to buy a drink for a complete stranger?*

Use a marketing message that intrigues them!

**Example 1:**

*Hi Ron. Nice to meet you. What do you do?*

*I am in the human jumper cable business.*

*Really?! Tell me more.*

*I work for Never Die Technology and it is our mission to get portable defibrillator units in every school and company.*

*I work for a school and we have been thinking about buying one. Got a few minutes to tell me more?*

Message sent, received, and understood!

*How do I get my marketing message across briefly?*

1. Engage the person who you are talking to.

2. Determine if continuing the conversation on a professional level is worthwhile.

If the person you are meeting and greeting knows that you are a valid supplier of something they need, that person will usually want to hear more. Therefore, your ability to communicate verbally (and in written form) a powerful message succinctly is absolutely necessary to maximize your networking and marketing opportunities.

**Example 2:**

*Ron, my name is Naomi. I am the CEO of Raelco. Who do you work for?*

*I help CEOs sleep better at night...but I'm not in the mattress business. Naomi, could you specifically identify who will be leading Raelco in 2012?*

*No. I do not think I could.*

*If you had that answer, I could bet you could sleep easier. I work with CEOs and boards who are concerned about who will be leading their organization five and even ten years from now. We work with you to identify and retain the people who will be there to make the tough decisions of tomorrow.*

*How do you go about doing that?*

I engaged Naomi, whom I had never met before, with a question. My message was tailored to her as a CEO. CEOs worry about retaining their key personnel. CEOs also are concerned about the leaders who will be retiring soon and who will replace them. Naomi also liked the "sleep better at night" reference.

*What do I communicate in my marketing message?*

1. The true value that you deliver through your products and services. This means stressing the benefits and value instead of the products themselves.

2. Who you best serve. Define in simple terms the niche or sort of client that you serve.

*How do I keep my listener's attention when networking?*

1. *Keep your message short*—Deliver your message or main point in 10 seconds.

2. *Use simple language*—Omit technical jargon and lofty language. Make yourself understood by anyone from a CEO to an eighth grader.

3. *Make the person think*—Cause the person to decide if they fit within the group you serve.

4. *Put your message to use*—The purpose of your marketing message is to use it in networking situations. Practice it until it feels right and then use it as your core message.

5. *Whenever someone asks*—"What do you do?" instead of saying, "I am an accountant," or "I am a CPA," give them your marketing message.

6. *Consider creating a second or third message*—Do this when you serve more than one market or provide more than one sort of value.

7. *If they ask you*, "How do you do that?" you made an impact on them.

**Example 3:**

*Hello Ron. Tell us what you do.*

*I put valuable business intelligence into the hands of decision-makers who must meet their customers' changing needs. My clients receive real-time information about what has happened, what is happening and most critical, what could happen. All of this wisdom on one page!*

*Really? Timely information is something that plagues me now. How do you go about doing this, Ron?*

I explained that value to them: business intelligence that tells of the past, present, and future. They listened to my marketing message and then qualified themselves because they had a problem that I know how to solve. Marketing messages are valuable, powerful, and free.

## 3. HOW TO CREATE VISIBILITY AND EXPERTISE USING SOCIAL MEDIA

### *Social Media Is Here to Stay*

This "thing" called Social Media feels like it suddenly appeared out of nowhere. Yet, Social Media and our reliance on it are in its early stages, and it will continue to evolve. For example, within the next two years, a majority of people and companies will use Facebook to send and receive e-mail!

Though Facebook Founder and CEO Mark Zuckerberg did not officially declare e-mail to be dead, he sees the four-decade-old technology as secondary to more seamless, faster ways of communicating, such as text messages and chats. In other words, Facebook is betting that today's high school students are on to something. "We don't think a modern messaging system is going to be e-mail," Mr Zuckerberg said at a special event in San Francisco.[1]

### Social Media Is Permanent

Yes, the importance and impact of Social Media is difficult for anyone older than 30 to understand, yet it is revolutionizing the way we communicate and interact, in both the personal and the business setting. As a Hired Gun, you must be prepared to adapt your work and marketing to this technology, and do so sooner rather than later. Other Hired Guns that you are competing against for part-time jobs or consulting opportunities have already adopted Social Media, and use it to create visibility and to find meaningful work.

Social Media is defined as "a group of Internet-based applications that build on the ideological and technological foundations of Web 2.0 and that allow the creation and exchange of user-generated content." This definition comes from "Users of the World Unite: the Challenges and Opportunities of Social Media" in *Business Horizons*, written by Andreas Kaplan and Michael Haenlein.

### Process of Social Media

An easy way to understand Social Media is to see what it can deliver for individuals, as well as organizations.

- *Conversing*—Communication using Social Media is about open dialogue. There is a public nature about the sharing of information, but the important aspect of it is that you can easily use tools to engage with the public at large. The old method was to send out spam and hope someone responded to you.

- *Listening*—With Social Media, you can tap into what your prospects or clients are doing and saying. The cost to do so is negligible. Prior to Social Media, it was very expensive to conduct a formal survey of prospects, but now, when a specific group or industry is using Social Media, you can tap into it easily to hear their conversations, concerns, pains, and the solutions they seek. When you have an understanding of your prospects' needs, you may be able to satisfy those needs for a single company or for an entire industry (community).

- *Channeling a Two-Way Dialogue*—A major aspect of Social Media, when compared to other forms of media, is that it can become an ongoing dialogue. To engage others using Social Media, you must be able to respond to their requests for information or comment. As you reach out to meet a prospect's needs, the engagement process begins. It is possible to develop a reputation as an expert in one particular area, and once you are recognized as one, others may proactively seek you out.

- *Providing Products*—Using Social Media you are able to quickly prepare digital or intellectual products and provide them to prospects at low cost. With the implementation and adoption of the Internet, however, many people expect stuff on the Web to be free. Therefore, in your business model as a Hired Gun, you can easily create digital versions

---

[1] NPR November 23, 2010.

of white papers, tools, checklists, or other value adding items that you must be willing to give away. Doing so can position you as an expert while opening the door for you to be invited in for a conversation about doing paid work.

On the Web, individuals and companies that drive to immediately charge for their intellectual property will be shunned! In most interest-specific communities, members flock to participants who provide valuable free services. By providing simple products for free, you will have the opportunity to market other products on a fee basis.

- *Sharing Resources*—Sharing hard-to-obtain information is one of the most important aspects of Social Media. You add value by sharing condensed information or brainstorming with other members of the community. You provide prospects and clients with informational links to such things as

  - Pertinent websites.

  - Book reviews.

  - Opinion pieces.

  - News articles.

  - Research data.

  - Videos.

  - Sites where you are highlighted as the expert.

### Goals of Social Media for the Hired Gun

The main point as Hired Gun for using Social Media is to establish thought leadership and credibility in a specific industry or among your peers. With it, you build relationships and loyalty of the target community toward your services or your brand. A Hired Gun like you can use Social Media as a tool to gather data and insights about your target market.

### The Many Applications of Social Media

The tools to use for Social Media continue to expand each day. However, here is a short list of what exists currently. You must understand and feel confident using each one. Some of them you are using, but maybe not in context of how to employ Social Media to market yourself broadly and easily as a Hired Gun and expert.

Social Media is found on tools and electronic platforms that serve as a hosting or routing source. Many of these can be found when you focusing on narrow interests, which allows you to hone in on a specific targeted group or community.

- *Social Content*—These are blogs and micro-blogs, podcasts, photo sharing sites, and video sharing sites.

  If you use or are familiar with Twitter, Flickr, or play games with other players remotely, then you are using this aspect of Social Media

- *Social Platforms*—These are communities, forums, or virtual worlds where people tune in to connect with their friends or other community members.

  If you have played any of the various SIMS games or use Facebook, Linked-In, My Space, Ning, Second Life, or Plaxo, then you are already using this form of Social Media.

- *Content Education*—These sites collect the syndicated web content and aggregate data into one location for you to easily review and access. This aspect also includes how-to and informational videos.

  If you have used or tapped into an RSS or feed reader, then you have used this form of Social Media. If you have searched for medical advice on WebMD, then you are familiar with its impact. Check out BillShrink, which is a source that people turn to for financial advice.

- *Reviews or Ratings*—Nearly every form of Social Media allows you to provide reviews or feedback on how well you liked the service or product. This tool is designed to provide other users with information to determine whether or not to follow your lead.

  One method of making a name for yourself is to be a regular reviewer of a particular product or type of services, such as restaurants, movies, hotels, or business books.

- *Resources*—This aspect of Social Media grows every day because of the growth in reference materials and tools.

  A few of the more common tools are Aardvark, Scribd, Slideshare, and Vimeo.

- *Media Management Tools*—Because the amount of tools and Social Media grow and expand exponentially, a whole new set of sites are developed to help you manage your personal Social Media easily.

  Ping.fm is one that I use, because with it, I can post one short message and the site is connected to 30 different Social Media formats. Check out these: Hootsuite, Tweetdeck, and Filtrbox.

- *Expertise Establishment*—Have you ever craved for media attention? You can create this attention, with persistence and effort, by subscribing to HARO, which stands for Help a Reporter Out. Similarly, Pitchrate allows you to make pitches, using your expertise. Subscribing to the The Huffington Post and commenting on articles positions you as "someone in the know." You can also post articles to Associated Content. Finally, check out how experts are positioned on JustAnswer.

- *Trend Spotting*—There is a plethora of sites that people use to make their opinion known. Beware: much of these sites contain the rants and raves of people with more time than sense. But, if you need to spot trends or need examples of what people think, you can tap into what is on people's minds.

  Reddit is one such site.

- *Seeking Out Contractor Type Work*—These sites come and go. But if you need cash or like to stay busy, check out Fiverr for very small projects. More formal bidding or project referral sites include Sologig, Consulting-Project, IFreelance, Freelancer, and FreelanceJobs.org.

### A Firm-Wide Strategy for Social Media

The first rule of using Social Media is to develop a goal and to incorporate it into your existing marketing objectives and strategies. For example, if you are trying to position yourself as an expert in venture financing or streamlined accounting, and currently write articles and partner with niche consultants, then your Social Media strategy should easily fit into your marketing efforts.

If you are an expert in not-for-profits, then you could use Social Media to continue to extend your brand and reputation, and even give back to your pet causes.

### Credibility

**Social Media can be either a credibility killer or builder.**

Today, if someone wants to find out something about you, they do not pay attention to your tri-fold brochure or your business card or other printed material. The first thing a potential client does is to Google or Bing your name and check out your website. If you lack a website that describes what you can do for the prospect, then you will likely not get many inquiries.

Beyond that, however, the main reason that people (who search your name or company on the Internet) do this is to check out your expertise. That is why having blogs, offering downloadable tools, and posting testimonials from previous clients pays off in establishing your credibility. If you fail to have a website, I guarantee that you will usually lack credibility.

That being said, a few of the successful Hired Guns I have met over the years did not have one, but they usually had a name or solid reputation in a specific industry or city, and they obtained leads and referrals solely based on their past accomplishments, exposure, or reputation.

### Benefits of Using Social Media

Besides the obvious win for you of lasting credibility, there are other benefits to adding Social Media in your marketing efforts. Here are a few:

- Becoming a Thought Leader through your expertise

- Client service

- Creating or increasing brand awareness

- Immediate comment or feedback

- Increased online identity

- Job or Opportunity Postings

- Market research

- Networking opportunities with other Hired Guns

- Relationships with traditional media outlets

- Search engine optimization

- Sources of revenue or opportunities to sell services

*Mistakes to Avoid*

Here are some major blunders that companies and individuals make when employing Social Media:

- Believing Social Media is a fad and will go away

- Ignoring the power and impact of Social Media

- Failure to stay in tune with changes and the direction of Social Media

- Failure to listen to their target audience

- Giving up on Social Media campaigns prematurely

- Not knowing where their target audience is or how to engage this audience

- Not measuring the results of their efforts

- Putting marketing ahead of providing information or creating dialogue

- Using Social Media without having a overall strategy

*Creating and Using a Blog for Visibility*

Each day over 10,000 new blogs are launched.

Business culture works on influence, authority, and relationships. People who have a strong and well-informed opinion command respect and become influencers.

The thirst for high-end business information, the kind that makes people feel like they are up-to-speed, created a $15 billion professional publishing market in the United States.

In business, being out of the loop means death.

John Battelle, Columnist for *Business 2.0* says, "Blogs will become a staple in the information diet of every serious business person. Not because they are cool but because those who do not read them will fail. Blogs offer an accelerated and efficient approach to acquiring and understanding the kind of information all of us need to make business decisions."

*Technology in Marketing*

Time is one of our most critical resources as a Hired Gun. Use technology only if it leverages your use of time, not usurps it. Remember, your objective is getting business. Examine whether your contact management system is helping you follow up and secure business or leaving you with less time to market.

Use your PDA for what it is best at:

- Tracking expenses,

- Recording contact data,

- Reminding you of tasks and due dates, and

- Giving necessary data on a prospect or clients.

Use your website for three purposes:

- Tell visitors of the value that you provide.

- Tell who said so through testimonials.

- Provide visitors with something of value for free.

### *How to Perform Anywhere Marketing*

Focus on

- Mobility.

- Agility.

- Rapid response.

- Access to resources to solve problems and get business.

### *Suggested Tools for Anywhere Marketing*

Tools for anywhere marketing include

- Mobile device with full Internet access

- PDA with contact management system

- Notebook (or smaller) computer able to perform word processing, spreadsheets, and sending faxes

- Powerful cell phone

- Web-based off-site storage for file sharing

## 4. HOW TO PARTNER WITH YOUR CLIENT FOR MORE OPPORTUNITIES

To successfully be seen as your client's equal partner in addressing their issues you need to manage and value these five qualities.

*Trust*

This is the glue of long-term profitable relationships. Be consistent in what you do and say. Doing so will allow your client partner to feel comfortable with you, because they know or can predict what you will do. Consistency engenders trust.

*Are you trustworthy? Are you consistent?*

*Responsibility*

This consists of two key words: response and ability. You must respond quickly to your clients' needs. You must have the ability to respond timely and appropriately.

*Are you able to respond and deliver what you said you could?*

*Sacrifice*

When you sacrifice for others, they lose the mindset that you are just out to take their money. Be willing to give something extra without looking for remuneration or reciprocation. The client took a risk in hiring you. Make sure their risk pays off in multiple ways.

*What little extras are you giving the client?*

*Mindfulness*

The basis for being a true professional is being mindful of others and their needs. A true partner thinks first of the partnership.

*Do you value and honor your partnership and your partner?*

*Passion*

You must have a passion for helping your client to be successful. Your passion needs to inspire them to take action.

*What impact do you want to have on your clients? Are you passionate about what you do? Does your passion show?*

Examples of Joint Venturing include

- You design accounting processes and team up with a Quick Books expert who does not do processes.

- Your prospective client has a complex tax situation that needs constant monitoring, so you partner with a CPA who sticks to taxes.

- You cooperate with a consultant who consults with CEOs on strategy but does not provide services such as budget preparation or scenario planning.

## 5. HOW A NICHE CAN ATTRACT OPPORTUNITIES

By positioning yourself or your firm into a discrete niche, you will always be guaranteed to have the highest rates, because when someone is in desperate need of the expert, they rarely question the amount the expert charges.

### *Niching Efforts that Pay Dividends*

Take the following steps to ensure that you make the most of your efforts to make yourself the expert at something.

Step 1: Tie Yourself to a Popular Cause

**Examples:**

Consult on

- Leadership succession planning.

- SOX compliance.

- Outsourcing.

- Distressed companies.

- Startups.

- Lean accounting.

- CEO roundtables.

Step 2: Play Up to Your Targets

Have ongoing dialogue with potential clients.

**Example:**

Create and use a blog.

Step 3: Spend Time Where Your Target Customers Are

**Example:**

Attend events where entrepreneurs are likely to be, then join and participate in organizations that your ideal client belongs to.

Step 4: Tailor Your Message for Specific Groups

**Examples:**

Industry-specific newsletters; custom mailings; tailored checklists; "Do you measure up?" pain tests.

Step 5: Listen and Adopt

Keep researching your target market to understand their changing needs.

**Examples:**

E-mail real-time articles; bookmark topic-specific sites; search through topic-specific directories to get an overview of what is available.

*Use Tools to Keep Informed about Your Niche or Expertise*

For up-to-date information on your area of expertise, try the following sites:

- www.refdesk.com
- www.factiva.com
- www.highbeam.com
- www.NYT.com
- www.daypop.com
- www.technovatis.com
- www.xanga.com (formerly Feedstar)
- www.kinja.com
- www.gawker.com

For free blog service, try this site:

- www.bloglines.com

*Niche Services You Could Provide*

Over the years I have met Hired Guns who built sustainable (and I assume profitable) businesses serving as

- Expert witness.
- Contract COO.
- Forensic accounting or auditing.
- CEO coach.
- Spreadsheet maven.
- Expert in HR manuals.
- Development expert for NFPs.

- Receivership consultant.

- Developer or author of business plans.

- CFO who attracts venture capital.

- Author or columnist.

- Seminar or webcast presenter.

And one dear to my heart,

- facilitator.

### *Viable Niche—Facilitator*

CPAs have a golden opportunity to be of service as a facilitator to their clients, because the work you do exposes you to many sorts of people, problems, and business situations. According to a 2003 AICPA survey, 90 percent of business decision-makers said that their accountant was competent, reliable, and demonstrated sound business judgment. Your CPA designation is a great piece of advertisement that shows you understand a business's needs for crafting real solutions.

### Keys to Being a Good Facilitator

Keys to being a good facilitator include

- *Meetings*—Every business meeting needs a leader, but not every leader is a good facilitator. Most executives are terrible facilitators because they lack the skills and because they have a stake in the outcome. There is a truism in business meetings: Once the CEO speaks, everyone stops sharing their thoughts and ideas.

- *Objective*—The facilitator's role is to be an objective third party in any group setting. The facilitator lacks an emotional investment in the outcomes or decisions. Your purpose is to ensure that the meeting's objectives get accomplished.

- *Involvement*—The facilitator's involvement can range from heavy to light. Your main responsibility is to foster dialogue among the participants so they share ideas, stay open to new possibilities, and make smart decisions.

- *Meeting Environment*—The facilitator's role is to create a meeting environment that is conducive to generating ideas for brainstorming and for honing those ideas with specific narrowing activities.

- *Fees*—Fees can range from a flat fee per meeting, to an hourly rate, and to a fee per attendee. You can bill on a project basis. Better yet, you can tie a fee for facilitation into your advisory, accounting, or compliance services.

- *Facilitative Situations*—The mere presence of an unbiased yet knowledgeable party helps to defuse negativity and prevents hurt feelings while encouraging involvement. As a facilitator, you can also challenge the status quo, prevent group think, or deter domination by one person or a minority.

Facilitators can be useful in any situation where people are called together to accomplish the tasks such as

- Generating ideas.
- Finding solutions.
- Allocating resources.
- Problem solving.
- Vendor selection.
- Retreats.
- Annual meetings.
- Budget or marketing strategy sessions.
- Budget resource allocation meetings.
- Company reorganization discussions.

All these require and benefit from an objective facilitator.

How to be Successful as a Facilitator

Upfront Skills

Facilitators need to enjoy being in front of a group, and need to have emotional maturity. You must be able to think on your feet, because you will often need to improvise when problems arise or people get off-track.

Emotional Intelligence

The facilitator must also be unafraid of emotional issues that crop-up in group dynamics. Your goal is to remove emotion out of a conflict and use it as a learning point. You help the attendees remain adults through their decision-making process.

Minimal Ego

The facilitator must use minimal ego. The meeting is not about you, it is about them. You are their process facilitator and are less important than the decisions and meeting outcomes. Naturally, as facilitator, you do not contribute to the ideas of the meeting. Instead, you keep the group on track to meet their goals.

CPAs who like to give advice and provide answers will not be successful as facilitators. Sharing your opinions—especially if you are highly regarded—will hinder your objectivity. Everyone loses when your ideas turn into their ideas.

To be successful in a retreat or brainstorming session, the ideas must originate from the group's attendees and not be introduced from the outside. This is another reason why most business executives make terrible facilitators.

### Shepherding the Group

The facilitator walks a fine line between letting the group explore and create and keeping the group on task. As facilitator, you must shepherd the group through the process and remove the barriers to their successful completion. If you drive them, they may not get to the most viable solution or stay accountable for the outcomes.

### Interaction

You must play well with others.

### How to Get Started as a Facilitator

1. Take a course or get a certification.

2. Offer your services pro bono to get the experience you need. Not-for-profits, homeowners associations, and local government units need but cannot afford professional facilitators. This effort creates visibility and cost-free-marketing.

3. Add Facilitator to your business card, website, and promotional material.

4. Co-facilitate with an experienced facilitator to practice and obtain feedback on your skills.

## Conclusion

**Stick to familiar turf.**

As the statement above suggests, stick to those things that you are familiar with when it comes to marketing your services. To successfully market yourself you do not need to change who you are. You do need to see yourself just a little bit differently. The selling of professional services is one of the hardest things for anyone to do because you are putting your reputation on the line. And, if you do not deliver what you promise, it will be difficult to convince others that you are good.

Therefore, in marketing professional services, *you must be good at what you do*. The mindset that you are an expert accounting professional who is looking for organizations that require your expertise will go a long way in helping you create opportunities and, more importantly, big fees.

The phrase stick to familiar turf reminds you to focus on the areas that you know best. If you have worked with small businesses, market yourself to small businesses. If you are an expert in cash flow management, market that service to organizations that need to manage their cash flow carefully. If you have a long successful track record of helping not-for-profits, then your reputation in the NFP community will help you gain clients. Most importantly, if you helped others to be successful, then you have the right to ask them to introduce you to their friends and colleagues.

Of all the skills that we cover in this book, the marketing of professional services will be the hardest to master. Do not let this discourage or stop you from being of service to others. With time and practice this skill becomes easier and easier.

# Chapter 8

# Resources and Concerns

**The story you tell others is what you quickly become.**

## Introduction

In this chapter, some of the common concerns about the role and responsibilities of the contract Controller will be addressed. Since there is no singular resource about this unique role regarding what to do and what to avoid, I researched and interviewed other contract Controllers. Much of this information in this chapter is the author's opinion backed by the experiences of those who also serve as Hired Guns.

Not every situation or issue that you face is covered in this book. The purpose of this chapter is to give you sufficient information so that you are both successful and able to share your wisdom with those who follow you. Much of this chapter will be in the form of questions.

The final proof if you are *doing things right* as the contract financial professional will be

1. You can sleep well at night without worrying about something you said or did.

2. You get referrals and repeat business.

After completing this chapter you should be able to

- Obtain answers to your concerns about the contract Controller role.

- Determine if you have issues about independence that need to be addressed.

- Help the employees you supervise become more productive and effective.

- Develop a model for setting your fees.

- Face up to the issue of ethics as a Hired Gun.

- Know where to turn if you have questions or concerns.

## What Other Things Do I Need to Know?

### *Do I Have Independence Issues to be Concerned About?*

The answer will depend upon several factors. The factors are whether

- You are doing the project through a CPA firm.

- You perform other accounting services as part of your Hired Gun practice.

- You use the CPA designation in your materials and communications.

- The client has sufficient accounting talent on board to prepare the financial statements.

In order to understand the issues, let us have a quick review of the basic rules that impact you.

## THE BASIC RULES REGARDING HIRED GUN INDEPENDENCE

1. CPAs must assess their independence if a financial statement is involved.

2. CPAs cannot attest to their own assertions.

3. An attestation requires independence.

4. CPAs cannot abdicate or ignore their commitment to professional standards.

### *Holding Out as a CPA*

"Holding yourself out" as a CPA means that you are employed by a certified public accounting firm or you provide services that a CPA firm traditionally provides. Some states regulations imply that if you have CPA after your name then you are holding yourself out. For AICPA purposes, using CPA on your business card does not mean that you will be automatically deemed a CPA firm.

### *Assertions*

Assertions are the opinions (or lack thereof) that CPA firms attach to the client's financial statements and projections. These include the audit opinion, review report, compilation report, OCBA report, and "I am not independent" statement.

## THE THREE TESTS

Whether you are independent or not depends on three tests.

Test #1 is to answer this question: "Do I use my CPA designation?"

As a Hired Gun you may retain your CPA license and take continuing education to retain your designation but this does not mean that you are holding yourself out as a CPA. The test is whether or not you have CPA on your business card, in your resume, on your website, and on your promotional material. If the answer is yes to this question, you must answer Test #2.

Test #2 is to answer this question: "Do I hold myself out as a CPA?" Do people understand that you are a CPA?

If you include it on your business cards and brochures then you are holding yourself out as a CPA. If you answered yes to this question, you must answer Test #3.

Test #3 is to answer this question: "Do I hold myself out as a CPA firm?"

This question determines whether you are acting like a CPA firm. If you provide any services that are provided traditionally by a CPA firm then you are one. This includes but is not limited to tax preparation and compliance, tax research, auditing, reviews, compilations, and accounting write-up work. Since most Hired Guns perform many related services—like tax filings—you are deemed to be a CPA firm. If you answered yes to this test then the rules regarding issuing a financial statement by a CPA firm apply. Any statement you take part in on the client's behalf, even if it comes off their accounting system is subject to some kind of attestation report.

Figure 8-1 graphically shows the three tests as steps.

**Figure 8-1: Three-Tiered Test on Independence**

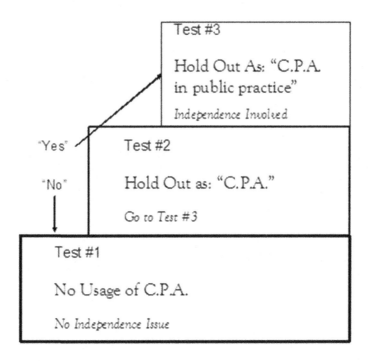

*I only do a limited number of tax returns for friends and family and do not charge anything. All of my income comes from being a contract Controller. Am I holding myself out as a CPA firm?*

The Internal Revenue Service considers you as a tax practitioner which means that others would as well. Since tax preparation is a service provided by a CPA firm you are probably holding yourself out as one.

*I am a CPA but I do not use that designation in any written material other than my resume. My clients never see my resume. Am I holding myself out as a CPA?*

Some folks will tell you that you are and others will not. The key test is whether your client understands that they are hiring a qualified CPA. Chances are during the interview or engagement process the subject of your CPA came up. Even if you do not use the CPA officially, the client knows that you are one. Consider yourself holding out as a CPA and answer Test #3.

*The subject of CPA never came up with my client and I do not use it on any marketing materials. I'm worried about my client's banker and not my client. Do I have an independence problem?*

At face value, you are acting only as a Hired Gun and not as a CPA firm. However, you do not know what your client said to the banker. He may have said to impress the banker, "I just hired a guy who's a CPA to serve as my CFO." The banker does not know of your employment relationship and may automatically assume that you represent a certified public accounting firm. Therefore you may be considered as holding yourself out as a CPA.

*The services I provide have nothing to do with accounting and I do not tell people that I am a CPA even though I retain my license. Am I holding myself out?*

As long as you are not using CPA in your marketing material or on your business card, then you do not have an independence issue and are not holding yourself out as a CPA—you meet Test #1.

*I work with companies in financial distress and act as their CFO as they go through liquidation or put themselves up for sale. Everyone knows I am a CPA, which opens doors for me. I do not prepare any financial statements or get involved with that process. Am I holding myself out as a CPA firm?*

You meet Test #2 but not Test #3. Helping companies in financial distress is not a traditional service offered by CPA firms. The fact that you are not involved with preparing financial statements also helps to alleviate the independence issue. Another factor is the client has accounting staff qualified to prepare financial statements and projections. If they do, you fail Test #3.

## Can I Issue Financial Statements as Their Controller or CFO? Do I Need to Attach an Attestation Report? Do I Need to Notify Lenders?

The issue of independence comes into play when financial statements are being issued external to the organization. In general, the rules are that if you are associated with a financial statement or financial projections you are required to add an attestation report to it.

After going through the Tests #1 and #2 and determining that you are holding yourself out as a CPA, then you need to address the issue of independence. Of course if you are holding yourself out as a CPA firm, you must attach some kind of report with the financial statements.

I have held a discussion about this topic with numerous experts and often receive conflicting advice. If you are serious about being a Hired Gun for the long term I suggest that you have in your library these documents: AICPA Professional Standards Statements on Standards for Accounting and Review Services as codified in the current Accounting and Review Sections; Rule 101 of the AICPA's Code of Professional Conduct; and Interpretation 101-3 "Performance of Nonattest Services."

*My only role is their CFO, in a contractor relationship. When I issue a financial statement for my client do I need to put any sort of report with it?*

This is a complex question for two reasons. At face value you do not need to attach any attestation report to the client's financial statement, should it go to a third party. However, there are other things to consider. Does the third party understand your role? Does the fact that you have CPA after your name lead them to think that you represent a CPA firm? Do you only take the data and prepare a financial statement without doing any analytical review?

Even though you are not required to do so I would suggest that you attach to the financial statement a letter detailing your responsibility in preparing it. You could, of course, add a compilation report to the financials stating that you are not independent, but by doing so you are putting yourself in the position of holding yourself out as a CPA firm. The letter that you attach to the financial statement explains that in your role as the CFO, you are preparing this statement for use by third parties. Even though you are a CPA acting in a contractor role, you do not make any sort of attestation to the contents or quality of the statement.

In general, think about how the other party may view you and your responsibility when issuing the financial report.

*I am a contract Controller and my client company issues statements to a bank and several outside investors. I take their data, put it in the general ledger, and do a few tests. Then I issue the financial statement on plain paper. Do I have to do anything else beyond that since I will not be associated with the report?*

This is the area where due care comes into play. Recently in Washington State a contract Controller found herself named as a defendant in a lawsuit for a company that failed. The CPA credential that is placed after her name leads to an assumption that she had certain knowledge about the business. She is being sued because the plaintiffs say she should have known enough to do some further checking. They are holding her to a very high standard, one that would normally be used against a certified public accounting firm. She did not include any sort of disclaimer with the financial statement.

This sad example illustrates why it is important that you not only use due care but also look at the situation through the eyes of the person receiving your client's financial statements. The fact that you are (or once were) a CPA carries a burden. When in doubt, always go for the highest standards available to you.

*I prepare internal financial statements for my client. Then I turn them over to the client's CPA firm who gives it their blessing. Do I have any concerns about independence?*

The concern here is whether the CPA firm issues an attestation report with the financial statement. If they do, you are functioning as the client's bookkeeper (no slight intended). If all they do is recommend adjustments to you, which you book, then you issue the financial statement on plain paper, your dilemma is that the CPA firm is now associated with the statement. You need to alter the arrangements with the CPA firm and require that they issue a report with the financial statements.

As you can tell from the questions posed in this and the previous section, you do need a good sounding board to raise these concerns. Many state societies as well as the IMA allow you to anonymously pose ethics questions and they offer their advice or recommendations. This may be a resource should you lack a group of colleagues who you can turn to.

## *In Essence*

Regarding the issues of financial statements and independence, do what helps you to sleep well at night. When in doubt, ask for help!

## Other Issues to Consider

### *Should I Specialize?*

In the Hired Gun field, it is better to be a big fish in a small pond than a small fish in the ocean. Specialists are the big fish while generalists are the small fish.

From my experience, the Hired Guns who make the highest amount of revenue per hour are those that specialize. Specialization allows you to get your name out more as the expert in that particular area. As we know, in business, experts command higher fees while generalists do not.

If you are unsure as to whether you have a marketable specialty, look back into your history and study all the types of firms you worked for and sorts of work experiences you acquired. Even better, talk to the people you worked for and ask them, "What do you think I am best at?" Their answers may surprise you and point you toward your area of specialization. We often fail to see ourselves as specialists, yet looking back at your history will show you that you have acquired a tremendous amount of expertise in one or more areas.

If you are considering this, pay close attention to this specialized marketing skill in the previous chapter.

### *Should I Sign Checks?*

If you are a regular employee in a part-time capacity signing checks is a natural responsibility. But if you are a contractor, *do not be a signer on any of the bank accounts.* You risk unwarranted liability if the client is doing anything shady. Your duties can include approving vendor invoices for payment, but that is where your responsibility stops. Require that an executive or officer of the organization sign all checks. The same rule applies to authorizing advances on debt accounts. Require an employee to do this.

### *Can I Sign the Payroll Tax Returns?*

Just like in signing checks, you incur a potential liability by signing these documents when you are in a contractor capacity. Part of your responsibility can be to prepare or review the various payroll and business tax returns. Have an authorized officer or executive of the organization sign the returns.

If there is a section on the return that reads: "Person to contact for questions," always enter a client's employee's name in that section, not your own.

### *How Should I Determine How Much to Charge for My Services?*

How much you charge will depend on several factors:

- Your expertise or specialty.

- The locale that you are in.

- The amount of competition you have.

- Whether other organizations are offering the service(s) that you provide.

- How you market or position yourself.

- How others market you.

- How your clients view you.

We accountants tend to minimize our self-worth and are willing to accept lower fees in exchange for staying busy. In the Seattle area a Hired Gun working on their own can be hired for as low as $25 and up to $200 an hour. In addition, a contractor who is placed through a recruiting firm such as Robert Half has a rate between $65 and $125 per hour. In smaller markets like cities in the Midwest, the hourly fees range from $25 to $100. In New York City the rates run from $75 and can go as high as $500 per hour.

CPA firms that sell their contract Controller services charge anywhere from $45 an hour to $200 or more.

One of the reasons for the fee differences is the client's expectation. Clients know that their CPA firm will charge them more than someone who is working on their own. Firms like Robert Half have published rates that are competitive.

The following is a suggestion for calculating your rate, which has two components:

- *Component #1*—Calculate, based upon local research, how much you would earn for that job (for example, CFO, accounting manager, Controller, and so on.) on an annual basis. Divide that salary plus benefits of about 35 percent by 2000. Then multiply that number by a multiplier from 1.25 to 2. That will be your Target Rate.

  | | |
  |---|---:|
  | Annual salary for a CFO in your market and ideal client | $120,000 |
  | Benefits and taxes add on 35 percent | 42,000 |
  | Total compensation | 162,000 |
  | Hours available for sale | ÷ 2,000 |
  | Rate 1 | 81.00 |
  | Multiplier | × 2 |
  | Target hourly rate (rounded) | $160.00 |

- *Component #2*—Check around your city or location to determine the range that the CPA firms are charging clients for the services that you will provide. Compare those rates with your target rate. Unless you have an expertise that the CPA firms cannot provide or you have a great reputation, your standard rate needs to be in line with the CPA firm. Similarly if you have recruiting firms in your city that provide contractors to their clients, determine the range of their fees.

- *The Multiplier*—The multiplier range is from 1.25 to 2.0. Intuitively you know the reasons for the multiplier. You will not be booked full-time. The time spent in marketing, billing, research, and education are all on your dime. Also, as a contractor you are responsible for your own taxes and, most likely, health benefits. The multiplier you use will be the one that you are comfortable with, based upon your self-worth and how valuable you are to clients.

Every Hired Gun has their personal philosophy on setting rates. They fall into three categories.

The first category are those who are unsure about their abilities and charge bookkeeping-level fees because they do not believe that they can get paid more. These are on the lower end of the scale.

The second category is those who are very sure about themselves and their skills. They make no apology for their fees and they always find clients who are willing to pay the fee requested. Their fees tend to be on the upper end of the scale.

The third category, the majority, is those that have a target rate somewhere in the middle and develop good negotiating skills so they charge close to that fee.

---

**Contractor Pricing Policy of Robert Half**

Pay scales varied widely, in the range of 110 percent to 250 percent of salary, with the agency getting a 30 percent commission off the top.

---

SOME TIPS ON HOW TO GET HIGHER FEES

Some tips on how to get higher fees include:

1. In your contract name specific points in time where you and the client will review the fee structure. Never go into an open-ended contract without this review because you may find that the work is much harder than you anticipated and you could be stuck with a low fee.

2. Get a retainer up front so that you work on the client's money.

3. Bill and get paid for your work in advance.

4. If the job entails a variety of duties, some at a basic level and some at a high level, calculate a blended rate that includes both.

5. Offer a fixed fee with a not-to-exceed number of hours. The reason clients often resist higher fees is because they fear the *Taxicab Syndrome*. If you help to alleviate their fear by capping what you will be charging them each month, the client will be more willing to pay your target rate.

6. Every one of us has in our mind how much a particular service is worth. So when you quote a rate that is higher than what your client feels that service is worth, then you must spend more time helping the client see the value that you are bringing to them.

7. Finally, go in front of a mirror and tell yourself your hourly rate. If you cannot do this without laughing, you do not feel that you are worth that amount of money. Change your attitude or change your rate.

FEEDBACK FACTOR IN FEES

**The client is lying when they say they cannot afford you!**

If they have a real need for the service, they have the money. They just choose not to pay it to you because your value proposition has not proven to them that you are worth your fee. This is the ugly reality that many consultants ignore and chalk it up to clients without money. This turndown is feedback that you have not proven the value that you can bring to the prospective client.

> According to Christian and Timbers, an Ohio based executive recruiter:
>
> Financial temporaries can earn between $200 and $500 a day depending on the local business environments and the consultant skills.

> David Maisler, Founder of Accountants 4 Contract said:
>
> "If we know that an assignment has long-term potential, we build in escalation clauses targeting fixed dates, such as six months or a year. On assignments that are time- indeterminate we periodically review and watch for changes in responsibility and scope. We try to peg rate changes to value added."

## Could I Take Stock in Lieu of Pay or Compensation to Help a Client Who Lacks Sufficient Cash?

This is not a good idea, because it not only affects your independence but it also puts you at risk for not getting paid for your hard work. It is better, in my estimation, to give back to the client through lower fees than to take an equity stake.

I have met a few contract CFO and Controllers who have done this. A CFO who I know does this because it is his specialty. He is connected to the venture capital market and his clients hire him because he can bring in venture money and help them develop a marketable business plan. He takes big risks. He now has an equity stake in some major Seattle companies and is very wealthy. Some other contractors have done this because they hoped to eventually become a part owner of the organization. In each case the person had other sources of income to fall back on.

## Do I Need Risk, Errors and Omission, or Other Insurance Coverage?

Since 1993 I have met only one contract Controller who felt he needed special insurance to protect himself. He would not disclose any details, but it sounded like he put himself in a high-risk situation. His personal insurance advisor suggested that he have the coverage. Except for errors and omission coverage, it is unlikely that you will find a policy that would cover someone who is an independent contractor. Unless you are offering advice to a client that has life or death implications—similar to a structural engineer—most Hired Guns say that you do not need to worry about errors and omissions insurance, while others disagree and purchase E&O insurance.

## Is There Any Insurance Protection That I Should Have?

There are four types of coverage to consider having in order to feel good about protecting your personal assets.

The first one is a general liability policy in the range of $1 or $2 million. In today's society people sue anyone with deep pockets for any reason. This protection has nothing to do with being a contract Controller and everything to do with living in a litigious society.

The second coverage to consider is to add on your auto insurance policy coverage for business travel and liability. Insurance agents tell me that if you are in a car accident and the other party discovers that you are traveling while conducting business, lawyers tend to sue you to get as much money from you as possible. It is common for business managers or executives involved in auto accidents to be sued for three to five times the amount of coverage in their auto policy.

The third coverage has to do with your homeowner's policy. Most likely you will have an office in your home. If you ever have a client or potential client over, you run the risk that they could be injured while in your home. You also may have some client documents on hand that could be damaged in a fire or disappear in a theft. You may have employees or subcontractors come into your home. For these three reasons, I suggest you talk with your personal agent and let them know what you are doing. They may recommend some additional coverage.

The fourth coverage has to do with disability arising from accidents that may occur at your client's workplace. As a contractor, you are not covered under your state's workers' comp program. If you are injured at your client's place of business, the client will claim that you are not eligible under their program since you are not their employee. Therefore, talk with your insurance agent to see if there may be some inexpensive coverage that will protect you if you are injured on the client's premises. In some states, like Washington, self-employed people can voluntarily opt into the state's workers' comp program. Check out the labor and industries program in your state to see if this is a possibility for you.

## What About Understanding and Using Technology?

You do not need to be an expert in technology, but you do have to keep up with some of the latest trends. If you consult with smaller businesses, they are years behind in the technology tools. One of the ways that you can add value to them is to offer suggestions on new tools that help their employees to be more productive and provide accounting data faster.

If the only computer technology that you use is always your client's, you run a slight risk of not qualifying as an independent contractor under the IRS rules. The independent contractor needs to have their own work tools.

The technology that you do need to become an expert at is on the tools that help you work anywhere. It is not unusual for a contract Controller who has multiple clients to spend hours each week in their car and at the local espresso stand.

## Can I Take the Home Office Deduction?

This is an issue that you need to take up with your tax advisor. (If you do your own taxes, have a conversation with yourself in the mirror.) About half of the Hired Guns I meet do take the home office deduction. The real issue that the IRS would raise in an audit is the fact that you do most of your work at the client's location. This would make it very difficult for you to justify an office in the home deduction.

## *Do I Need My Own Contract?*

Those accountants who have been contracting for a while usually end up having their own contracts. Some have written their own and others have consulted with an attorney to develop one. Some use an engagement letter similar to ones used by a CPA firm.

If you work for an organization that uses contracted employees regularly, like Microsoft, they will give you their own contract to sign. This happened to me in my first stint as a contract CFO. My client handed me a 35 page document and asked me to sign it. My jaw dropped to the floor—I was not expecting that! After that experience, I developed a proposal format that includes a scope of work attachment. Then the proposal and scope of work become my contract that I have the client sign.

Remember two key issues regarding contracts:

1.  Having your own contract shows that you are serious and handle things professionally.

2.  Contracts are only useful when things go wrong. That is the point in time when you need to worry as to whether you have adequately covered yourself and your rights.

## *How Does the Issue of Ethics Impact Me or My Role?*

There is no uniform Code of Conduct that consultants must follow. If you have a designation such as a CMC (Certified Management Consultant) or are a member of an organization such as the IMA, AICPA, or your state society, you must abide by their ethics. Codes of Conduct are basically reminders to act professionally.

If you are not subject to any codes of conduct like those mentioned above, then follow these guidelines and you will not have any concerns about your conduct regarding ethics:

*   Never commit to doing something that you do not have the ability to do.

*   Never lie to a client or make up credentials you do not have.

*   If you feel uncomfortable about the situation, then pursue the reason for your discomfort—your body never lies.

*   Deliver what you promise and do not promise what you cannot deliver.

*   Be willing to walk away when the client shows you that they do not live up to high ethical standards.

*   Always use due care.

*   Always stay objective.

*   Avoid the merest hint of a conflict of interest.

*   If you work with others, employees or associates, determine if they live up to high standards.

- When in doubt, talk the issue over with trusted colleagues.

- Never let your ego interfere with good business judgment.

## *What Are My Risks?*

**Everything in life contains risk. Risk has both an upside and a downside.**

Here are some risks to consider as you make your choice on whether or not to be a contract professional. As a Hired Gun you risk

- Liking what you do.

- Not liking what you do.

- Taking on more work than you can handle.

- Not earning enough income.

- Creating a positive reputation.

- Building up a viable business.

- Disappointing a client because of other commitments.

- Not getting paid for the work you do.

- Feeling alone or working in isolation.

- Having to invest in your own professional development.

- Taking on a project that requires more work than you expected.

- Having a long list of satisfied clients.

As you can see from this list none of these risks are insurmountable. Ultimately you must review your life's goals and decide what you want to do to earn money and to contribute back to the society.

## *Do I Need to Worry about Independent Contractor Status?*

RULES FOR INDEPENDENT CONTRACTOR

The IRS has 20 different factors they look at to determine whether a person is truly an employee or an independent contractor. The formal determination is made using a form SS-8.

*The Keys to Ensuring That You Stay an Independent Contractor Are:*

- Have a written agreement stating your relationship.

- Have the right to control the means and manner of the service.

- Subject yourself only to expected results. You control your processes.

- Make sure you are not economically dependent on the one entity you work for.

- Supply your own equipment, tools, or supplies.

- Do not let the client set your exact hours. Specify that you can perform services outside of the normal working hours.

- Obtain a state tax identification number.

- Provide for payment by a retainer, by milestones, or upon completion of the project. Avoid hourly billings, if possible.

- Invoice for your services and expenses. Never use the client's expense form.

- Provide that the relationship can be terminated upon breach of the agreement.

- Do not prepare the same regular reports that employees are required to submit.

- Do not expect payment for training from the client.

- Never fill out the client's employment application form.

- Provide the client with a form W-4 and request that they issue you a form 1099 Misc. at the end of the year.

By following these suggestions, you will avoid having to prove that you are a contractor instead of an employee. You will also help your client avoid this too.

## *As a Consultant, Are There Any Problem Areas to Avoid?*

PITFALLS OF CONSULTING

The pitfalls of consulting include:

1. Consultants make too many promises and end up providing too few deliverables.

2. Consultants promise unique, customized advice but produce cookie cutter solutions.

3. If a project succeeds, the consultant takes all the credit. If a project fails the blame belongs to the client.

4. Some business leaders, desperate for a quick fix may implement good advice and then abandon the solution when it does not produce dramatic results within a few months.

5. Executives, when faced with a controversial or unpopular decision, will hire consultants. When the consultant's advice backfires or people are unhappy with the change, executives have a built in escape hatch and a handy scapegoat.

6. A chronic dependence on consultants usually indicates a chronically weak leadership. Approach these clients with caution because this client often leads to pitfall 5.

## *Is It Wise to Supervise Employees When I am Only a Contractor?*

(If you are a part-time Controller, not under contract, this issue does not apply.)

The easy answer is no. However, there will be things that you must consider such as the length of the project and whether or not someone else can fill the role of supervisor. In my first Hired Gun project, I was asked to supervise five people. The person they reported to on paper, the President, did not have time to do any hands-on supervision. So as their CFO (under contract) I agreed to supervise them. Luckily for me these five were self-starters and just needed someone to bounce ideas off of and give support when it was needed.

Some Hired Guns tell me that they will not take an engagement if it includes supervisory duties. Others go with the flow of the assignment.

Assuming that in your role as contract Controller you are asked to supervise employees, tell the client up front that you will do it, but some of the traditional roles of a supervisor will need to be performed or filled by others. An example of this is the screening process of new employees. You do not need to be involved in every interview during the hiring process.

Assuming this is a longer term project of more than just a few weeks, you will quickly be able to size up if there is someone else in the accounting department who could take the role of lead or acting supervisor. A lot of supervisory tasks are time consuming and this is the reason that you need to limit your responsibilities in this area.

### PERFORMANCE EVALUATIONS AS A CONTRACTOR SUPERVISOR

An issue regarding supervision that I needed to address in my first role as a contract CFO was to conduct performance evaluations for my five direct reports. They complained that they had never received any sort of evaluation, mainly because the President was not in touch with what they did.

My approach was to make it a group evaluation. I prepared a questionnaire and gave it to each employee that my staff member regularly interacted with. I then compiled their feedback and used that information as my performance evaluation. In effect, I was not the evaluator, their peers were: I was the messenger, the interpreter, and the person they could talk to.

If you need a tool to conduct a performance evaluation, in the Appendix of this workbook is a best practice tool. It is titled the "Learning Curve Performance Evaluation." I use this tool to help employees quickly master their job and shorten the learning curve of their responsibilities. I include it because, if you work for a smaller organization or dysfunctional company, they probably lack adequate performance evaluation tools.

One of the biggest issues that you may face, especially if you walk into a mess, is raising employee performance. In the section following this, there are some suggestions on how to do this. The key to raising employee performance quickly is to use performance metrics.

ELEVATING EMPLOYEE PERFORMANCE QUICKLY

Companies skilled in performance measuring use specific metrics to drive their productivity increases. They ask themselves: "What behaviors or actions do we need to measure to increase the likelihood that we will achieve our performance and productivity goals?"

The purpose of this best practice is to get you to apply metrics that will enable your employees to be more effective and productive in their day-to-day work. When employees understand exactly what is expected of them in terms of accomplishments and know that they are being constantly measured they become more effective, productive, and stay accountable.

In this best practice are tools that set goals and standards for each employee so that they understand your efforts to help them become peak performers and know that you will reward and recognize them for their efforts and contributions.

Let us begin your understanding of this best practice by going into some key terminology.

*Employee Performance Defined*

Performance related to the employee can be defined as how well the employee does their job against the expectations placed upon them. Employees who are considered peak performers have a reputation for exceeding these expectations, while the underperformers' reputation is for not living up to the minimum expectations. As a supervisor, your responsibility is to create peak performers or replace those people who are unable to become star performers.

Employee performance issues are based on the assumption that the employee has the ability to perform at higher levels of quality and productivity, but is choosing not to.

*Employee Productivity Defined*

Productivity or effectiveness is putting in effort so that the results exceed the effort. It requires that the employee does the right things, instead of being efficient, which is doing things right!

Accountants say they want efficiency. If you fall into that trap, you are barking up the wrong tree. To be efficient, you demand that everyone cross all their T's and dot all their I's without regard to whether their work adds value to your customer. Being productive, on the other hand, is paying attention to what the customer expects and moving heaven and earth to meet that expectation.

> **Employee Performance Lesson: You cannot affect an employee's performance until you can accurately describe it to them clearly.**

EMPLOYEE PERFORMANCE PRINCIPLE 1

- In the absence of honest feedback, employees will make up their own standards for acceptable behaviors and performance. Their standards will never be higher than yours.

## Advice from Experienced Hired Guns

> Micah McCracken, President of Tatum CFO Partners
>
> "Your network should not be just for the contacts to get the next job, but to have access to the expertise you need in your [current] job."

### *Paul Colao Is a Contract CFO*

"I introduced myself around to venture capitalists figuring they could use my financial expertise." Paul worked on an interim basis with venture capitalists helping them in the early stages of financing for promising startups.

### *Erin Corsair Is a Professional Temporary*

"Since all of my projects are strategic, involving short-term problem solving, I am never bored."

### *Curt Halin Is a Contract Controller*

"I am trying not to compete with the CPAs in public practice. Clients benefit the most when I am able to work with the CPA firm." Curt says the average length of his assignments is six to nine months and only one in ten clients will remain as a long-term engagement with continuing monthly needs.

Curt finds new clients through referrals, cold calling, advertising in the Yellow Pages, and personal contacts. "I cannot overemphasize the value of networking and persistence. Once you have a lead you should begin to develop a relationship with the decision maker of that organization. It could easily require three or more contacts and as much as a year before the potential contact turns into a client."

"I will only be able to handle two or three major clients at one time." Usually a new client has an intense need, so he works at their office two to four days a week for several months. Then the time commitment drops off. Once that client's needs are met, he can move on to the next client crisis.

Curt's advice to you:

- Develop a business plan.

- Network extensively within your business community.

- Get to know other consultants.

- Keep your billings up to date.

- Contact attorneys who deal with small business and bankruptcies.

- Clearly and carefully describe the services you agree to perform.

- Develop a long-term perspective.

## *Bob Anderson Chooses to Niche in Retail*

Bob has been a Hired Gun for 15 years and worked in or with the grocery industry long before contracting. His "typical engagement is 3-4 days and longest engagement is working part-time for 3 months." Bob markets his services by direct marketing with phone and in-person meetings.

The one thing that Bob wishes he had known when first starting out was the need for "diversification in clients." The grocery industry is consolidating and his typical client—the small retail store—is becoming scarce.

Bob's advice to you: Do not let it [the job] consume all your time. It is negative to other clients.

## *Scott Allred Is Located in Montana and Relies Heavily on the Internet to Provide Services*

Scott defines his services as "CFO Solutions" or "Controller Solutions" depending on the needs of the firms he has targeted. "I started providing outsourced accounting services in August of 2002. The services were provided using trained staff, internet technologies, and other state of the art software. As clients used our services, I found myself providing additional services in the Controller and CFO job description." Scott, similar to around 30 percent of Hired Guns, incorporated his business because of the concerns for liability and hiring his own employees.

Scott decided not to niche but does target specific markets. "At this point I provide services to a broad spectrum of clients, from storage facilities, dentists, computer firms, and manufacturing." His current challenge is: "To provide a consistent product and to do so in a timely fashion. Because of this limitation, it is important to have a solid system in place. This is the system I am working on, but is not a two hour project."

In marketing he found that direct telephone telemarketing works for him and so does obtaining referrals. Scott is developing a new website designed to sell his services using a "master sales page." He believes there is success in using this approach.

Scott has had up to eight client projects going on at one time and his typical engagement consists of recurring annual engagements. His longest engagement has been 3.5 years and still going.

The one thing that Scott wishes he knew from day one is: "Marketing, marketing, marketing. I have spent a lot of capital with a lot of things not working."

Scott has advice for those starting out as Hired Guns

- The skills you will need to rely on most are
    - Communication.
    - Developing a Job Description.
    - Planning.
- Make sure you have the personality and people skills to make it work.

- Understand the personalities of those you are working with. Some may not be worth the anxiety and trouble to work with them, even if it means you have some income.

- Have a good plan for transitioning into an engagement. There is nothing more frustrating for you and the client than to have the process stalled or on a slow track.

- Learn your job and perform your services very well in less than 3 months.

- Offer a guarantee that has some teeth to it.

## *Gene Siciliano Is CFO for Rent®*

Serving clients through his firm CFO for Rent, Gene considers himself to be the godfather of the contract CFO, since he has been doing this work for 21 years. The clients Gene serves are CEOs of privately owned companies in the lower end of the middle market; mostly manufacturing, service, and some distribution. Gene added another revenue source by offering a finance coaching service for senior executives of large companies. Gene never felt the need to incorporate his business even though he has employees, two under contract.

His main challenge is in being "a single shingle coping with the swings in revenue and still saving enough to build net worth for later years." As he blazed the trail for the rest of us, Gene found that a "good stream of referrals, my CFO for Rent brand, my principal website, my people skills, my consistent follow up on leads, my published book, and to some extent my speaking are the ways new clients find me." Gene's firm has two websites and is working on a third.

Regarding engagements, Gene says he serves 5 to 10 clients at a time with the average length of a typical engagement being 6 to 12 months. Asked about his longest engagement, he told me: "A current client is now in their 4th year; their 3rd was their best profit year ever." Sounds like Gene's advice pays off.

The three critical skills that Gene relies most on to remain successful are

- "Pretty good marketing sense—the ability to create and implement marketing ideas that raise my visibility; the fact that I genuinely like people adds to the appeal, I think."

- "Strong communication ability—I project a credible image during sales calls, and make my competence AND communication ability clear to the prospect. I listen well and prospects and other professionals see that. I often have a close after a single meeting."

- "Financial management skill—the technical core of my trade. I am a strong accountant, a skilled financial expert, and a good judge of talent in the financial area."

This long-time CFO has these words of wisdom for those starting out. "The larger the average size of your client, the larger the average size of your invoice. Owners and CEOs of small companies agonize over paying for professional services, while professional managers of large companies take it as a cost of doing business. Find a unique niche, become an expert at it, and find a way to brand your approach to that niche. Hire a marketing expert to help you exploit it, because you cannot do it yourself, even if you worked in the marketing department of XYZ before. Do this as soon as possible."

## *Audrey Godwin Defines Herself as a Chief Business Integrator*

If you want to see a professional contractor's website that attracts attention, you need to visit Audrey Godwin's. Audrey's experiences in both public accounting and then in industry prepared her for the role she plays with her clients when she founded her firm, the Godwin Group. "I have had my own firm for four years and before that was an employee of other firms for 4 years. I have been doing this work for 8 years."

"I refer to myself as a CPA and business advisor. I also say that as CFO I am the Chief Business Integrator, since I understand the different dynamics in a business and can speak to everyone from the owner to the sales manager to the receptionist in a way that is useful to the sustainability of the business. I serve clients who have annual revenues of under $5 million. They are primarily in the construction and real estate development industry, business service professionals (graphic designers, copywriters, and so on.) and some retail."

Audrey's firm is a PLLC. We did this "mainly for cash flow reasons since the company is still in growth mode. This allows me to take draws when needed and not be hooked into a salary and related payroll taxes." Her firm currently has two employees.

As of now Audrey is managing 3 CFO projects, 10 Controller engagements, and her longest engagement is serving as a CFO in a situation moving into its second year.

Her ongoing challenge is the one that almost all Hired Guns face: "Being a sole practitioner, staying motivated and connected to colleagues. I enjoy 'group think' from time to time just to gauge where I am and to see what I can leverage from others. Educating smaller clients that they cannot afford not to have me as part of their management team." Audrey spends considerable effort to help potential clients see her as more than a tax CPA.

Audrey asked me to pass these pearls of wisdom to those who are interested in this role. "Evaluate your soft skills. Do you listen well? Are you okay with not being the expert, but being a facilitator and coach? Invest in personal development classes to enhance your soft skills." The one thing she wishes that someone would have told her when she first started is "that it would take a good two to three years to create an educational awareness campaign to help business owners understand the role of the CPA outside of taxes."

Networking and speaking engagements are Audrey's paths to new clients. "I belong to associations that are directly related to the industries I serve. I do workshops and seminars related to business development and management so it shows my expertise in this area."

The three skills she relies on most are

- Active listening.

- Creativity.

- Critical thinking.

## *Sandra Copas Owns a Firm on the Leading Edge*

Sandra is doing something that is nearly impossible in the Hired Gun business: partnering with her husband, Bryan, in a firm that generates sufficient work for both of them and other Hired Guns. (Most married couples find it impossible to work with their spouse and still stay married.)

Sandra and Bryan's firm only started in August of 2004, but they are evolving the firm to meet their clients' changing needs. Regarding the firm's specialties Sandra told me, "Most Hired Guns work offsite. We believe our clients receive a greater benefit from us being at their place of business. We offer business advisory services in addition to controllership or CFO work—HR support, meeting facilitations, assisting in the creation of a vision, business plan—which allows us to give our clients help in areas that may be overlooked. Many business owners believe their only problem is financial. Typically, multiple issues need to be addressed. Our consultants must have significant experience, education, and training. It is most effective when the senior level financial manager who understands, for example, the treasury functions of individual clients, is watchful of fraud, and knows how to run a successful business."

"To be cost effective, our [ideal] clients must have revenues over $1 million (but $2 million is preferred) up to $20 million, employs less than 15 people, needs less than 25 hours of work for their controller or CFO, per week, *and* have some knowledge of how to run a business. It is surprising how many businesses fit the first three criteria but not the last."

"The maximum number of clients that one consultant can handle is 8 to 10 per week, working half-days. Our engagements are ongoing with 6-month contracts. Our longest engagement is almost 2 years and still going."

Sandra is always concerned about marketing. "Educating potential clients and our lead generators is our biggest obstacle. It is difficult for a layperson to explain (sell) or understand (buy) our value proposition." Besides having a website, Sandra and her partner spend time being visible to potential clients. "What works best for us are networking, direct mail campaigns, and online advertising."

The three critical skills that she tells me you need to remain successful are

- Lifetime learning.

- Effective listening and communication skills ranging from the most basic to highly technical or professional.

- Networking.

If she were to look back to when she first started, Sandra said the one thing she wished someone had told her was, "If something feels wrong from the start, do not accept the engagement. Use intuition when accepting new clients. Do not accept every prospect who asks for help."

Sandra passes on this advice to you. "It is important to know how to run a business, not just the numbers. Communication skills must be excellent. Unlike tax work, clients will not see instant improvement. Constant and regular communication with the client is essential to manage the project and keep the client happy."

## *William Looney Left the Corporate Big Company Environment after 20+ Years*

Bill was burned out from the never ending cycle of downsizing and working harder but not smarter. He launched his firm in 2004 as an LLC, which gives him the benefit of a 401K plan. Eschewing a fancy title, Bill refers to himself a Consultant or Contractor.

Bill's niche is the industry he worked in. "My work centers from my experience as a general accountant and controller in a manufacturing setting. Based on that I am able to do accounting related project research, temporary employee coverage (due to personnel transitioning between assignments or taking on personal leave of absence), account analysis and reconciliation cleanup (monthly or year-end). I have also been involved in analyzing operational mill level financials for litigation support. All my work so far has been with forestry and wood products related companies. The average length of an assignment is slightly over one year, though I had one short term assignment that was based on a single project approximately 1 month in duration. My longest assignment lasted 14 months."

His litigation support is high value, high paying, and hard work but it is not without challenges. He is most concerned about "not giving in to anxiety regarding future assignments; personal marketing to a broader market; managing multiple client obligations."

Bill is honing in on his approach to marketing and does not have a website or even a business card yet. Not from neglect, but from picking up work the minute he put up his shingle! So far the personal contact is working to bring in meaningful work to him.

Since Bill feels that he is still in the start-up mode, his advice to you is fresh in his mind. "Make sure to cultivate personal contacts and build on core strengths and abilities. I would also recommend a strong financial position to have the confidence that cash reserves provide." His initial concern was "that I would be fully engaged on a steady basis." He now realizes "how critical personal contacts are in obtaining assignments."

"The three critical skills I rely most on to remain successful are

- Analytical ability.

- Controllership or General Accounting experience.

- Skills using Microsoft Office products to produce analytical models, budgeting worksheets, reconciliation tools, and presentations. Also, I have an ability to learn, use, document and train others on a variety of financial software packages (Sage products, People Soft, CT3, and so on)."

---

**Activity 8-1 : What Contributes to My Success?**

Think about some ways that you specifically

- Stay focused.

- Keep your eyes on the big picture.

- Retain Teflon-coated mental toughness.

Think about things that serve you well.

---

*(continued)*

*(continued)*

> - Tools to help you remain productive.
>
> - Tools to market yourself.
>
> - Other tools you rely on.

## Controller's Resources List

These are the books that I found very useful in helping me to add value as a Controller, especially in the areas of assisting clients to do a better job of reporting.

- *Performance Scorecards: Measuring the Right Things in the Real World*
  Richard Y. Chang and Mark W. Morgan, Jossey-Bass
- *The HR Scorecard*
  Brain Becker, Mark Huselid, Dave Ulrich, Harvard Business School
- *Balanced Scorecard Step by Step: Maximizing Performance and Maintaining Results*
  Robert S. Kaplan and David P. Norton, John Wiley and Sons
- *The Balanced Scorecard: Translating Strategy into Action*
  Robert S. Kaplan and David P. Norton, Harvard Business School
- *Built to Last: Successful Habits of Successful Companies*
  J.C. Collins and J. L. Porres, Harper Collins
- *The 80/20 Principle: the Secret of Achieving More with Less*
  Richard Koch, Doubleday Dell Publishing
- *High Performance Benchmarking: 20 Steps to Success*
  H. James Harrington and James S. Harrington, McGraw Hill
- *Keeping Score: Using the Right Metrics to Drive World-Class Performance*
  Mark Graham Brown, Quality Resources
- *The Profit Zone: How Strategic Business Decisions Will Lead You to Tomorrow's Profits*
  Adrian Sluwotzky and David Morrison, Three Rivers Press
- *Profit Patterns*
  Adrian Sluwotzky and David Morrison, Times Business Press
- *Women Lead the Way*
  Linda Tarr-Whelan, Berrett-Koehler Publishers
- *See Jane Lead*
  Lois P. Frankel, Business Plus

These are the ongoing resources that I found very useful as Controller. They helped me see beyond my job.

| Publication | Publisher | Frequency | Contact Information |
|---|---|---|---|
| *C.F.O. Magazine* | The Economist Group | monthly | www.cfo.com |
| *Business Finance* | Duke Communications | monthly | www.businessfinancemag.com |
| *Strategic Finance* | Institute of Management Accountants | monthly | www.strategicfinancemag.com |
| *Fast Company* | Fast Company | monthly | www.fastcompany.com |
| *Workforce* | ACC Communications | monthly | www.workforcemag.com |
| *H.R. Magazine* | Society of Human Resource Managers | monthly | www.shrm.org |
| *Technology Review* | Technology Review | bimonthly | www.techreview.com |
| *The Cost Controller* | Siefer Consultants | monthly newsletters | www.siefer.com |
| *CFO and Controller Alert* | Progressive Biz Public | bi-monthly | www.pbp.com |

### Providers of valuable services to Controllers

| | |
|---|---|
| Institute of Management Accountants | www.imanet.org |
| Balanced Scorecard Consortium | www.balancedscorecard.com |

# Chapter 9

# Take the Next Step

**"The toughest thing of success is that you got to keep on being a success."**

**Irving Berlin, composer**

## Introduction

After completing this chapter you should be able to

- Spot trends that impact our profession.

- Use trend analysis to look for opportunities to serve clients.

- Determine what your next step will be.

## Opportunities Abound

As you come into the end of this book, you may begin to feel overwhelmed about the task ahead in becoming a contract financial professional. Please realize that many others have gone before you and have successfully made the transition. The best place to start is with a personal commitment to learn and take more risks.

This chapter contains a tool for you to use in your commitment to grow. In addition, if you need more reasons why you need to add value to your employer or clients, study the trends that are impacting every Controller and CFO throughout the United States. Just as the quotation at the top of this page reminds us that there is work required to stay on top, keep in mind that you must commit to becoming more effective. Despite any trepidation or fear that you may feel, remind yourself often that once you have made the transition to become a part-time or contract Controller/CFO, the rewards you receive will be tremendous and far outweigh the challenges you face.

The many significant trends will help you see that there is a world of areas that you could specialize in to make money, have multiple clients, and satisfy your need to contribute.

---

**Self-Assessment #6: Mistakes Made By Controllers and CFOs**

Your friend Pauline made many of these most common mistakes. At a coaching session, as a way of reminding her that she is human, you tell her about the mistakes you made along the way.

**I made the mistake of**

\_\_\_\_\_ Not taking on the role that my company or client needed of me.

---

*(continued)*

*(continued)*

| | |
|---|---|
| _____ | Not recognizing the power and influencing aspects of the Controller's role, as the conscience of my organization. |
| _____ | Not creating a team approach but instead trying to do it all by myself. |
| _____ | Not becoming an equal participating member of a leadership team. |
| _____ | Not recognizing the value and importance that office politics—corporate culture—plays in making things happen. |
| _____ | Not becoming a sales person for myself, my needs, and my team's contributions. |
| _____ | Not growing as an articulate communicator and tough negotiator. |
| _____ | Not looking toward the future and the changes in the accounting profession. |
| _____ | Not adding value to my clients in numerous, visible, and measurable ways. |
| _____ | Not creating a network with other Controllers or CFOs with whom I can share ideas and offer or get support. |

*Which of these have you made?*

*Which of these have you made more than once?*

*Which of these have you learned from and changed your ways?*

## Five Accounting Leader Realities

In addition to the pitfalls to avoid, these are five realities that you must face in order to make yourself and your team more effective. Most are self-explanatory, but I have added a few comments at the end. The "we" is you, your team, and our profession.

- Unless we change our thinking, tomorrow looks just like today.

- Without a clear vision of tomorrow, what we expect tomorrow will not change from today.

- If we raise our expectations, we alter our future vision.

- Our skills and knowledge grow obsolete at an ever-faster rate.

- A finance/accounting team only advances in two ways: 1) the solutions we provide, and 2) the connections we sustain.

### OUR SKILLS AND KNOWLEDGE GROW OBSOLETE AT AN EVER-FASTER RATE

You must devote the time and resources to training and educating your staff. The skills you and your team acquired as recently as three years ago are now outdated. Even if your employer does not provide you with the funds for training, you must find ways to get your people trained.

## A FINANCE/ACCOUNTING TEAM ONLY ADVANCES IN TWO WAYS: THE SOLUTIONS WE PROVIDE, AND THE CONNECTIONS WE SUSTAIN

As accountants we are very good at finding solutions and very poor at maintaining connections. This is an area that you will need to focus a lot of your attention to. The connections I refer to are

- Getting outside of your office and meeting with people, face-to-face, on a regular basis.

- Making allies with your peers on the executive or management team.

- Becoming part of a networking group.

  **Rule of thumb:** As the Controller you need to spend 25 percent to 35 percent of your time meeting with those you serve, including major customers, investors, creditors, and of course your peer managers.

  **Rule of thumb:** Your employees must spend 10 percent to 15 percent of their time outside of the accounting department, meeting with those they serve (for example, vendors, customers, bankers, service providers, coworkers, and peers).

## *Significant Trends in Accounting Impacting the Controller*

Be sure to refer back to the trends regarding being your own employer and boss, highlighted in chapter 1.

*What trends do you see occurring in business?*

*What does the future hold for accountants?*

TREND #1

### The Cost of Processing Transactions is Approaching Zero

This is characterized by the information illustrated in table 9-1.

**Table 9-1: Comparison of Labor Cost Per Transaction**

| Finance Process | Cost in the Average Company | Cost in the Worst Company | Cost in the World Class Company |
|---|---|---|---|
| A/R remittance processing | $0.67 | $13.68 | $0.01 |
| P/R check processing | $1.91 | $10.93 | $0.36 |
| A/P invoice processing | $2.93 | $6.80 | $0.35 |
| Tracking fixed assets | $4.05 | $19.10 | $0.16 |
| Expense report processing | $6.05 | $25.75 | $0.27 |
| | **Labor cost per transaction** | | |

Source: *AICPA and the Hackett Group www.thehackettgroup.com*

Notice how close the costs in the last column are to zero.

TREND #2

### Everyone Demands Instant Gratification

This is characterized by the following

- The Internet and World Wide Web.

- WiFi availability.

- Cable TV, CNN, satellite radio.

- Quicken and QuickBooks.

- Executives who can get information on demand anywhere anytime yet have to wait 10 days for accounting to issue reports.

TREND #3

### The Finance Group Will Spend Less Time Processing and More Time Consulting

This is characterized by the following

- Decentralization of controls and management reporting.

- Demand for real-time financial results.

- World-Class companies are able to close within one day.

- Finance must track, measure, and report on nonfinancial data.

- Time spent processing transactions must be reduced below 35 percent from its current 77 percent.

- Widespread adaptation of the scorecard and dashboard for internal reporting.

TREND #4

### The Finance Group Will Be Ever Smaller and Less Permanent

This is characterized by the following

- The average finance group is between 33 percent to 70 percent smaller than it was 25 years ago for the same size of company.

- The typical manager's span of control is approaching 25 employees (it was five employees in 1970s).

- For every U.S. worker who loses their job, there are 25 employees who would leave their job if they could afford to.

- The average salary and benefits of an American worker in industries (where jobs are being added) is $22,000 and where jobs are being eliminated is $32,000.

- CEOs will continue to use downsizing and outsourcing as a permanent management tool.

TREND #5

**A Finance Professional's Employment Will Not Be Full-time or "Permanent"**

This is characterized by the following

- Today's college graduate will have 5 to 8 different careers and spend 20 percent of their time unemployed before they retire.

- U.S. companies are relying on just-in-time employees to meet any growth in employment.

- Contingent workers make up between 25 percent to 33 percent of this country's workforce and will grow to 50 percent by in the next decade (contingent worker = part-timers, contractors, and leased employees).

- 91 percent of businesses use temporary employees, which resulted in the temporary industry to grow tenfold over the last ten years.

- 30 percent of all new jobs created are part-time and lower pay scale positions.

- American businesses are outsourcing finance and administrative work in record numbers.

TREND #6

**Movement Toward a Pay for Performance Compensation System**

This is characterized by the following

- Wage increases to professionals that are barely keeping up with inflation.

- Employers demanding that employees must provide positive proof that they are earning their compensation.

- Profit sharing plans and stock options are replacing annual raises.

- "What have you done for me lately" mentality widespread among executives and managers.

- For many professionals, 20 percent to 30 percent of compensation is based on performance milestones.

TREND #7

**Accountant Required to Have a Broader Base of Knowledge beyond Accounting/Finance**

This is characterized by the following

- Almost all of accounting is done using technology.

- The profession requires a five year degree in order to become a CPA.

- During a merger the employees who are retained are those who have skills beyond accounting.

- Continued outsourcing of non-value work like A/P invoicing, collections, receipts processing, and tax preparation.

- By the year 2020, 75 percent of all American workers will need retraining because their skills have become obsolete.

- Technology's life cycle hovers around 18 months.

TREND #8

**Reliance on Tasks Forces and Project Teams**

This is characterized by the following.

- Work is being characterized as a series of projects staffed by employees whose expertise is required to bring the project to fruition.

- Due to poor communications, there is more reliance placed on cross-functional task force and project teams to get the work done.

- CEOs screen for accountants who can work well with others and are team players.

- Just-in-time employee syndrome.

- A majority of employee teams have members in remote sites or locations.

TREND #9

**Increase in Need for Compliance and Governance That Does Not Waste Resources**

This is characterized by the following.

- Sarbanes Oxley.

- U.S. workers who admit doing slow, sloppy work on purpose—currently 22 percent and rising.

- Current and past scandals for financial reporting, stock options, and the *pro forma* earnings. The next scandal will be hedge funds.

- More and more reliance on technology instead of people to make decisions and process transactions, leading to lack of awareness on the quality of the work.

- Executives who put profits ahead of governance.

- Greed.

- Achieve sales targets at all costs.

- Ends that justify the means.

- "What have you done for me lately" mentality widespread among executives and managers.

> **Answer These Questions**
>
> How will these trends impact your clients in the future? How are they impacting now?
>
> How will these trends impact you and your team?
>
> How will these trends impact your career?
>
> Do you see other Accounting trends?
>
> Which trend will have the biggest impact on you? Why?
>
> How can you best start preparing today for tomorrow?

## Tool: Instilling a Personal Commitment

> **Exhibit 9-1**
>
> **Personal Commitment Form**
>
> I commit to taking these actions, and I will check back with myself to verify that I have done something on or around _____ (follow-up date).
>
> Date prepared _____
>
> My signature _____
>
> My accountability partner is _____
>
> I will check in with my accountability partner every _____ days.

> **Activity 9-1: What Is Your Next Step?**
>
> Now that you have lots of information about how to add value to your clients, while boosting your career, it is time to figure out the next step. Complete your own action plan.
>
> *What is your future vision about your role as Hired Gun six months from now?*
>
> *What are you willing to do to improve your role as a shaper of your own future?*
>
> *What will be the long-term payoff for the changes you are going to implement?*
>
> *What will you specifically need in the future?*
>
> - Coach _____
> - Mentor _____

*(continued)*

*(continued)*

> • Specific training _____
>
> • More support _____

## Tool: Instill Continuous Improvement

The Plus/Delta Analysis is an excellent learning tool for every meeting, project, or performance evaluation.

The Plus/Delta Analysis is a summary of what is worth repeating and what needs improving. It spawns rapid improvements, shortens the learning curve, and increases accountability.

> **Exhibit 9-2**
>
> **The Plus/Delta Tool**
>
> | Pluses ✚ | Deltas ▲ |
> |---|---|
> | (Things that work and should be kept) | (Things that need to change or be better) |

### *Steps of the Plus/Delta*

1. Announce to everyone the purpose of the Plus/Delta.

2. Spend time gathering a list of things that worked well and list them on the Plus side. Stay with it until this list is complete or there are no more suggestions.

3. Spend time gathering a list of things that people would like to see changed and list them on the Delta side. Again, stay with it until this list is complete or there are no more suggestions.

4. Before the next session or meeting, address the changes that were previously recommended and accommodate those that cannot be changed.

5. Start the next meeting by reviewing the most recent Plus/Delta.

6. Remind everyone that you will continue doing what is working from the Plus list.

7. Inform the team of the changes that will come from the Delta list.

8. Explain which changes cannot be implemented, then brainstorm alternatives.

9. Continue to use the Plus/Delta tool at each meeting, event, or gathering.

10. Notice and celebrate how quickly improvements are taking place.

   **Note:** This is good documentation to retain for demonstrating to others that you are being proactive in addressing people's suggestions for improvement and are listening to your best resources. Even better, it models for clients what it takes to be an agent of change.

> **Activity 9-2: Application Step**
>
> How will you use the information you learned in this book?
>
> How will it help you in your own career?
>
> Who will you network with to keep your energy and focus tuned in?
>
> How can an experienced mentor help you?

## Conclusion

### There is a real need for your services!

The need is expected to continue to grow dramatically because of ongoing reengineering, pressures to lower costs, and the new paradigm of the flexible organization. *Consultants flourish when companies are confused, anxious, or optimistic about the future.* Hired Guns like you love to take on problems that have multiple layers of complexity.

### *The Challenges of Being a Part-Time or Contract Controller are Many*

- Produce quick results.
- Limited time and income.
- Super-high visibility.
- Few external rewards for achieving success.
- Unreasonable expectations on you.

### *But There are the Upsides of Opportunities Too*

- Personal autonomy.
- Flexibility.
- Doing work that is fun, fulfilling, and challenging.
- Higher income.

### *You Can Increase the Odds of Your Success If You*

- Hone your skills as a negotiator, time manager, and delegator.
- Identify opportunities for yourself before launching into the role.
- Define your role through a Position Description.
- Stay focused, know what is important, and establish priorities.
- Keep your eyes on the big picture.
- Be accountable for your results and success.
- Think in terms of systems to support what the company needs.

- Think in terms of systems to support what you need.

- Market from your strengths.

- Build your own support system or network.

- Leverage your time and knowledge.

# Appendix A

## Best Practice Tools

*Best Practice: Learning Curve Performance Evaluation*

This tool is to be used for evaluating an employee's performance on a Learning Curve basis. The ratings shown are designed to highlight the employee's current status on mastering the critical aspects of their job.

The tool fosters a dialogue about expectations with the employee because it highlights misunderstandings or miscommunications about the skills and abilities necessary to be a valuable employee.

INSTRUCTIONS

1. In the Performance Criteria column, list the specific skills, responsibilities, or duties that the employee must master in order to be successful in the position. Be sure to refer to the employee's latest Position Description and update the PD as needed.

2. Complete the Supervisor's Assessment page by circling the appropriate learning curve measurement for each Performance Criteria. Be sure to think carefully about all the elements of that skill, including special nuances. Be sure to consider whether the employee has consistently demonstrated the ability to fulfill the Performance Criteria since the last evaluation.

3. Provide the Employee's Assessment page to employees and ask them to complete it, focusing on where they see themselves on the learning curve for each Performance Criteria.

4. Compare the differences between your assessment and the employee's. Be prepared to discuss all discrepancies, especially those that are significant (i.e., vary by more than one point).

5. In the face-to-face evaluation meeting, ensure that the employee fully understands what you expect of them in each Performance Criteria.

6. Discuss and describe any new Performance Criteria that will enable the employee to grow and develop.

7. End the evaluation session with a specific Action Plan on how the employee will move up the scale on each Criterion.

**Supervisor's Assessment**

Rating definitions:
0 = Employee has yet to start or learn due to time or other constraints beyond his or her control
1 = Employee is in the initial stages of learning or undertaking this aspect of their job
2 = Employee has started work on this and has significantly more to learn
3 = Employee is performing right on schedule or meeting my expectations
4 = Employee is performing faster or better than my expectations
5 = Employee has mastered this criteria
6 = Employee is exceeding my expectations in this aspect of their job

| Performance Criteria | Assessment of the employee's learning curve for each criteria | | | | | | |
|---|---|---|---|---|---|---|---|
| | Yet to start | In the initial stages of learning | Started and significantly more to learn | Performing right on schedule | Performing faster or better than expected | Mastered the criteria | Exceeding expectations |
| Ability to communicate with coworkers | 0 | 1 | 2 | 3 | 4 | 5 | 6 |
| Ability to communicate with supervisor | 0 | 1 | 2 | 3 | 4 | 5 | 6 |
| Ability to audit for errors and omissions | 0 | 1 | 2 | 3 | 4 | 5 | 6 |
| Cross-trained on A/R function | 0 | 1 | 2 | 3 | 4 | 5 | 6 |
| Ability to set daily and weekly goals | 0 | 1 | 2 | 3 | 4 | 5 | 6 |
| Ability to complete goals | 0 | 1 | 2 | 3 | 4 | 5 | 6 |
| Ability to work unsupervised for long periods of time | 0 | 1 | 2 | 3 | 4 | 5 | 6 |
| Contributing ideas on a regular basis | 0 | 1 | 2 | 3 | 4 | 5 | 6 |
| Ability to prepare understandable spreadsheets | 0 | 1 | 2 | 3 | 4 | 5 | 6 |
| Ability to think strategically | 0 | 1 | 2 | 3 | 4 | 5 | 6 |
| Understanding of screens related to A/P and GL | 0 | 1 | 2 | 3 | 4 | 5 | 6 |

**Employee's Assessment**

Rating definitions:

0 = I have yet to start or learn due to time or other constraints beyond my control
1 = I am in the initial stages of learning or undertaking this aspect of my job
2 = I have started work on this and have significantly more to learn
3 = I am performing right on schedule or meeting the expectations placed upon me
4 = I am performing faster or better than the expectations placed upon me
5 = (I believe) I have mastered this criteria
6 = (I believe) I am exceeding my supervisor's expectations in this aspect of my job

| Performance Criteria | Assessment of the employee's learning curve for each criteria | | | | | | |
|---|---|---|---|---|---|---|---|
| | Yet to start | In the initial stages of learning | Started and significantly more to learn | Performing right on schedule | Performing faster or better than expected | Mastered the criteria | Exceeding expectations |
| Ability to communicate with coworkers | 0 | 1 | 2 | 3 | 4 | 5 | 6 |
| Ability to communicate with supervisor | 0 | 1 | 2 | 3 | 4 | 5 | 6 |
| Ability to audit for errors and omissions | 0 | 1 | 2 | 3 | 4 | 5 | 6 |
| Cross-trained on A/R function | 0 | 1 | 2 | 3 | 4 | 5 | 6 |
| Ability to set daily and weekly goals | 0 | 1 | 2 | 3 | 4 | 5 | 6 |
| Ability to complete goals | 0 | 1 | 2 | 3 | 4 | 5 | 6 |
| Ability to work unsupervised for long periods of time | 0 | 1 | 2 | 3 | 4 | 5 | 6 |
| Contributing ideas on a regular basis | 0 | 1 | 2 | 3 | 4 | 5 | 6 |
| Ability to prepare understandable spreadsheets | 0 | 1 | 2 | 3 | 4 | 5 | 6 |
| Ability to think strategically | 0 | 1 | 2 | 3 | 4 | 5 | 6 |
| Understanding of screens related to A/P and GL | 0 | 1 | 2 | 3 | 4 | 5 | 6 |

> ### Action Plan for Growth and Development
> This is where the supervisor suggests and the employee agrees to take specific steps to improving their performance and speeding up the employee's learning curve.

## *Best Practice: Probing Questions*

HOW TO GET TO THE REAL PROBLEM WHILE BUILDING TRUST

The consultant uses probing questions to uncover the client's pain. You are like a doctor poking around the patient's body. You poke and prod until the person says ouch. This is where you need to start whenever seeking a solution.

The reason you act like a doctor is because the person who needs a solution knows there is a problem and is unable to resolve it on their own. They have a goal or destination that they want to get to. Not being able to get there leaves them very frustrated, so they naturally are defensive. If you use direct questioning, you will only spark them into a defensive posture, leaving them unable to explore the real causes for their pain.

Probing questions are critical to the Controller or CFO because they

- Get people to think and unlock untapped potential.

- Allow people to discover their own answers, thus transferring ownership.

- Mine the real experts (the employee or manager) for their gold.

- Help people realize how the work they do contributes to the whole.

- Help people feel fulfilled, satisfied, and valued.

- Build positive attitudes and self-esteem.

- Remove blocks and open people up to unexplored possibilities while inviting discovery, creativity, and innovation.

- Help people envision what it will take to do what has not before been attempted.

- Guide people toward where they want to go, while recognizing the value in where they have been.

- Involve people in the decision-making process and generate commitment to solutions.

- Generate alignment with a shared vision or desired outcome.

- Encourage people to identify, clarify, and express their wants and needs.

- Encourage people to take risks.

- Recondition people from knowing what to think to knowing how to think.

A-4

- Nurture a deeper relationship and engender trust.

- Dissolve resistance to change.

- Create a high-energy, high-trust environment.

*Fundamentals of Probing Questions (PQs)*

- PQs are open-ended.

- PQs ask "What" or "How" instead of "Why" or "Who."

- PQs are YOU oriented.

- PQs show that the questioner is open and willing to hear the answer—whatever it may be.

- PQs are framed to fit the situation and clarify what is required.

- PQs help people learn through the process of answering.

- PQs give the person credit for their answer whether they know something or not.

- PQs cannot be answered "yes" or "no."

- PQs use a layering technique.

- PQs require advanced preparation.

- PQs start out general and then get specific.

---

**Examples of Structured Probing Questions**

Assume that you are trying to understand why an employee has missed a deadline or does not appear to you to take an Action Plan seriously. You would naturally want to hold this person accountable. If you start the conversation out with confrontation, the employee will become defensive and may not be honest about this situation. Try using these questions to uncover and understand all the facts so you can enable the employee become part of the solution.

Ask the employee:

*What is already working well?*

*What makes this project viable?*

*How are you doing on achieving your goals in the Action Plan?*

*What are the benefits of achieving your specific objective?*

*How can I help you in accomplishing your Action Plan?*

---

*Why Accountants Fail to Use Objective Questioning*

For whatever reason, built into the personality structure of the person drawn to accounting is the desire to get to the bottom-line fast. So the questions we ask others to help get there are often pointed and are filled with assumptions about the situation. While this approach may seem economical and timesaving, it is rarely effective.

The following change agent skills rely heavily on probing questions:

- Active listening.

- Objective observing.

- Testing your assumptions.

- Integrative thinking.

- Selling ideas.

- Tenacity.

- Intuition.

You start by asking questions that are general in nature and then move to more specific ones. These latter questions get you to the heart of the matter or issue. The tone of your questions needs to show that you are open to listening and desire to find the cause of the issue without specifically blaming the person you are questioning.

People naturally or habitually go for expediency rather than objectivity.

Printed in the United States
By Bookmasters